# Building a New Church

## A Process Manual for Pastors and Lay Leaders

*James E. Healy*

*Foreword by Nathan D. Mitchell*

## LITURGICAL PRESS
Collegeville, Minnesota

www.litpress.org

1    2    3    4    5    6    7    8

**Library of Congress Cataloging-in-Publication Data**

Healy, James E.
    Building a new church : a process manual for pastors and lay leaders / James E. Healy ; foreword by Nathan D. Mitchell.
       p.    cm.
    ISBN 978-0-8146-3269-7 (pbk.)
    1. Church facilities—Planning.   2. Catholic church buildings.   I. Title.
BV604.H43   2009
254'.7—dc22

                                             2009005100

# Contents

Foreword by Nathan D. Mitchell   v

Preface   ix

Acknowledgments   xi

1. *Who, Us?* An Introduction   1

2. The Roles of the Pastor   5

3. Assessing the Need   12

4. Parishioner Communications   20

5. Selecting an Architect   26

6. Selecting a Fund-Raiser   32

7. Parish Strategic Planning   38

8. The Architectural Master Plan   45

9. The Financial Feasibility Study   51

10. The Liturgical Education Process   55

11. Church Visits and Assessments   64

12. Developing the Design of the Church   67

13. The Capital Campaign   83

14. Construction—Getting Underway  93

15. Interior Decor and Furnishings  98

16. Original Artwork  103

17. Landscaping and a Prayer Garden  111

18. Construction Wrap-Up and Loans  118

19. The Dedication Ceremony  127

20. Conclusion—Reflections  135

List of Appendices  139

------------

*Appendices are available online only and are downloadable free of charge at http://www.litpress.org/new_church.*

1. A Possible Steering Committee Structure
2. Demographic Formulae
3. Possible Homily Topics with Suggested Outlines
4. Architect Interview Form
5. Architect Interviews Compilation Form
6. Fund-raiser Interview Form
7. Fund-raiser Interviews Compilation Form
8. Strategic-Planning Survey
9. Acoustical Consultants Interview Form
10. A Sample Feasibility Study Questionnaire
11. Church Visits: Church Assessment Form with Design Guidelines
12. Church Visits: After-Mass Reflection Questions
13. Sanctuary Floor Plan: Some Geometry Reminders
14. Value Engineering Worksheet: Evaluations and Prioritizations
15. A General List of Church Furnishings
16. Artist Interview Form
17. Artist Interviews Compilation Form
18. Loan Calculation Spreadsheet in Format for Excel
19. A Basic Checklist of Ministries Needed for the Rite of Dedication
20. The Rite of Dedication from the Roman Pontifical

# Foreword

*Nathan D. Mitchell*

Whenever a parish takes up the challenge to build, renew, or redesign its worship space, it inevitably has to deal anew with its own identity as church. As the bishops of the United States wrote in their statement *Built of Living Stones* (BLS; approved November 16, 2000), "one of the most significant and formative experiences in the life of a parish community is the process of building or renovating a church" (BLS, preface, 1). This means that the process of church construction or renovation is never a utilitarian (often contentious) act calling only for ad hoc decisions about fund-raising, creating finance and facilities committees, choosing an architect, or hiring contractors and engineers. It is a theological enterprise, a spiritual journey. Designing and building spaces and furnishings where the Christian assembly will meet its God in repeated, hospitable acts of washing, anointing, forgiving, marrying, burying, eating, and drinking is faith in action—it's theology with skin on.

BLS also reminds us that church building or renovation offers a parish the opportunity to review its own history, to reacquaint itself with the basics of liturgical theology, to strengthen and renew its identity as a community of faith, love, service, and witness to Christ's abiding presence within the world's tumultuous history (see BLS, preface, 2–3). For, as the Canadian Conference of Catholic Bishops points out in *Our Place of Worship* (OPW), "a church building is never merely functional; it points beyond itself to convey something about God.

Building, art, and furnishings function symbolically when they share the quality of 'transparency,' revealing the Creator behind the created object" (Ottawa: CCCB, 1999, p. 9). The Canadian bishops go on to suggest that every parish planning to build or renovate spaces for liturgical celebration must deal with three questions: *Who are we? What do we do together?* and *What environment do we need* in order to show clearly "who we are" and "what we're doing" (see OPW, p. 9)? These three questions, the bishops note, are best answered when the community listens attentively to three *voices*—those of the *local parish church*, of the *Church at large*, and of the *physical environment itself* (ibid.).

These three questions—and the three "voices" that help us answer them—are front and center in Fr. James Healy's invaluable guide to the pastoral processes involved whenever a parish tackles the task of building a new church or renovating an old one. In this brief foreword, I will outline five principles that, in my view, may show us how the "voice of the Church at large" can—through its accumulated wisdom, experience, insight, faith traditions, and theological reflection—help local parishes articulate *"who they are," "what they do together,"* and *"what environment"* best shapes their common faith and worship. These principles are embedded especially in the Second Vatican Council's Constitution on the Liturgy (*Sacrosanctum Concilium*, SC), in its Constitution on the Church (*Lumen Gentium*, LG), and in the most recent edition of the *General Instruction of the Roman Missal* (GIRM 2002).

• *Principle 1*: **The church is a people before it is a building**. We sometimes forget that one of the charges made against the earliest Christians was that they were "atheists," i.e., they seemed to have no visible "gods" or "places of worship," no "public sacrifices" (such as those offered to the Roman emperor), and no "officiating priesthood" (such as the one that ministered at the liturgies of the Jerusalem temple). Christians seemed to gather and pray wherever and whenever it was possible or convenient—in homes, in synagogues, in upper rooms, in prisons, in public squares, on street corners. Moreover, the apostle Paul insisted that the church is not a place but a person, the Body of Christ, member for member. This distinctive identity of the Christian people was highlighted in Vatican II's Constitution on the Church, *Lumen Gentium* (LG). There the world's bishops asserted that the church is first of all a mystery rooted in God's own inner life (LG, chap. 1), and that from this mystery flows its identity as pilgrim People of God (LG, chap. 2). In short, the church is not primarily an institution, a geopolitical entity, or a juridical organization, but a living, squirming people called into being by God's Word and sustained in communion by the Holy Spirit.

• *Principle 2*: **Worship spaces exist to serve the assembly's liturgy, not vice versa**. Although environment (space, furnishing, ritual objects such as ambo, altar, and font) inevitably shapes the assembly that uses it, the "full and active participation by all the people is the paramount concern, for *it* is the primary, indeed the indispensable source from which the faithful are to derive the true Christian spirit" (SC 14; emphasis added). Action trumps aesthetics—or to put it better, the *primary* aesthetic of the liturgy is God's holy, pilgrim people actively participating in the central sacraments of our salvation. We do not (or should not) hold worship spaces hostage to a particular "iconographic program" or to a particular "staging arena designed for choir, organ, and instrumentalists." Every church's best iconography is the people who worship there (shabby, soup-stained, and wrinkled though they be), just as its best music is the assembly's song (even when it sounds loud, puny, dull, or off-key).

• *Principle 3*: **Participatory liturgy requires a participatory church**. When the bishops at Vatican II voted to restore the people's rightful role in the liturgical action—and when they chose to define the church primarily as "mystery" and "pilgrim People of God"—they made it clear that ecclesiological models that concentrate decision-making power in the hands of clerical leaders alone are no longer adequate. This is surely one reason why, in OPW, the Canadian bishops insist that the *voice of the whole local church* is essential (not optional or merely "decorative") for determining who we are as God's People gathering, regularly, to celebrate the Mystery of Christ. The call to holiness, the call to mission and ministry is universal in the church, a consequence of our baptismal incorporation into Christ through the gift of the Spirit, his "first gift to those who believe" (Eucharistic Prayer IV).

• *Principle 4*: **Christian worship is not "altar-centered" or "ambo-centered," but both**. "The two parts which . . . go to make up the Mass, viz. the liturgy of the word and the eucharistic liturgy, are so closely connected with each other that they form but one single act of worship" (SC 56). The "two tables" (of God's Word, of Christ's Body and Blood) are not rivals or competitors but are "mutually implicative," each evoking and calling forth the other. In our worship, we are simultaneously a people who gather in contemplation around the Word and who share the "one bread and one cup" that makes us "the one body of Christ, a living sacrifice of praise" (Eucharistic Prayer IV).

• *Principle 5*: **Finally, Christian worship is the starting point, not the destination**. Liturgy is activity with a profoundly eschatological character; it is "food for the journey," but not the journey's final goal. Our destination is God's kingdom (reign, rule), that new creation that gathers all peoples of all times and places into the "wedding feast of the Lamb." As John tells us in the book of Revelation, "I also saw the holy city, a new Jerusalem, coming down out of heaven from God. . . . Behold, God's dwelling is with the human race. He will dwell with them and they will be his people and God himself will always be with them. . . . He will wipe every tear from their eyes, and there shall be no more death or mourning" (Rev 21:2-4; NAB).

In sum, our liturgies, humble and bumbling as they often are, exist for the sake of that heavenly liturgy where God, our gracious Host and Guest, welcomes us home, invites our friends, kills the fatted calf, puts rings on our fingers and festive clothing on our bodies, and says, "I have never left you; I have loved you forever; you are engraved on the palms of my hands; and whenever you call me, I will be there." This is our common destiny, rooted in our common baptismal vocation. "Without the faith assembly," OPW tells us, "ministries are pointless. When the assembly gathers to express its faith in a public way through its liturgy, the risen Christ in the power of the Holy Spirit is active amongst the community to lead it in worship of the Father. Each member, endowed with gifts of grace, 'one having one kind and another having a different kind' (1 Cor 7.7) shares the Christian vocation to build up the body of Christ by using his or her particular gift for the common good" (OPW, part 1, p. 11). That is who we are. That is what we do. That is why our church buildings are never mere meeting halls; they are the space where "God is dwelling with the human race," wiping every tear away, destroying death, and bringing us together to the banquet of everlasting life.

*Nathan D. Mitchell, PhD, teaches liturgical studies in the Department of Theology at the University of Notre Dame and is concurrently an associate director of the Notre Dame Center for Liturgy.*

# Preface

This book is written out of the ecclesial experience of an author in the Roman Catholic faith tradition. The references here reflect that denominational affiliation, its terminology and theology. These references are not meant to exclude any readers of other denominations who may benefit from the ideas and processes contained herein. Rather it is the intention of the author that as many people as possible from other faith traditions have access to this material.

Consequently the reader's indulgence is asked when confronted with Catholic terminology. Simply translate such Catholic terms into your own denominational language as is necessary (e.g., *priest* to minister or pastor; *parish* to congregation or church assembly; *parishioners* to congregants or church members; *diocese* to judicatory or regional church authority; *Eucharist* or *Mass* to the Lord's Supper or worship service, and so forth). As for the theology, particularly in chapter 10 on liturgical education, readers of different denominations should substitute their own theology of liturgy and worship, using their own denomination's documents and guidelines.

A cautionary word about hierarchical processes and authorizations. Diocesan procedures for building churches can vary greatly from diocese to diocese. Be sure to check with your diocesan officials at the outset of the planning process so you are clear on what they require from your parish. Other denominations who use this book as a guide also should check with their respective judicatories about their building procedures.

The term *steering committee* evolved during our own building project and stood for the separately created lay leadership group that, with the pastor, business manager, and director of parish liturgy and music, literally steered the parish through those many processes, decisions, and tasks of building a new worship space.

In a genuine ecumenical spirit, it is the hope of the author that other denominations and congregations, their pastors, and lay leaders will find these processes and suggestions valuable along their own journey of building a new church.

# Acknowledgments

In addition to the entire staff at St. Mark the Evangelist Parish in Independence, Missouri, the author would like to express his personal thanks to Gayle LaPlante, business manager of the parish at the time of the building project, and to Susan Walker, director of liturgy and music during and after the construction of the new church. The new church would not have happened as well and as beautifully without you. Thank you.

To Denis Greene of The Church Development Foundation (TCDF. org), my personal gratitude for his early and consistent encouragement in the writing and development of this book and for his counsel about the chapters on selecting a fund-raiser, parish strategic planning, the financial feasibility study, and the capital campaign. This book would not be a reality without your support, Denis. Thank you.

To Leon Roberts, construction and real estate manager of the Archdiocese of Kansas City in Kansas, my genuine appreciation for his technical expertise on matters architectural and beyond. I am especially indebted for his counsel regarding the chapters on selecting an architect, the architectural master plan, acoustical consulting, and specific elements of the pastor's role. Your experience as an architect and your dedication to the church have been inspiring. Thank you.

A special thanks to Ryan Bodenstab for the geometric illustrations in appendix 13.

*Chapter 1*

# *Who, Us?* An Introduction

If you are glancing at this volume, then some part of you suspects, if not already knows, that building a new church might be in your future. Your response to that prospect may range from *Oh, Boy!* to *Oh, God!* to *Who, Me?* If you have been around the church very long at all, it is natural that your response might be found somewhere along a spectrum running from elation to fear to questioning if you are the right person for the job.

*Oh, Boy*, a chance to correct all the errors I've seen and experienced in the churches built by others. *Oh, Boy*, an opportunity to make a mark, to leave a legacy, to help enshrine a faith community's values.

*Oh, God*, a future filled with endless meetings. *Oh, God*, parishioner squabbles over everything and being caught in the middle. *Oh, God*, the dreaded fund-raising, finance committees, and more hassles.

*Who, Me*, I am not qualified to be on a new church building committee. I am just an ordinary, everyday member. *Me*, I don't know if I can or want to. Does the pastor know who is being chosen for this job? I'm just not sure.

Questions and hesitancy, whether by a pastor or a parishioner, are normal. In fact they are healthy, for if there were none you might be the subject in the axiom about rushing in where angels fear to tread. So let me take a moment here at the beginning to address some of these concerns, both of the pastor and of the parishioner being asked to serve on this building committee.

1

First, the pastor. If you have some miles on you as a pastor, then I'm guessing there are more *Oh, Gods* than there are *Oh, Boys*. In fact you may have already tried to locate the phone number of the personnel board chairman. You might be having some thoughts like these: "I'm not a builder, not one of those bricks-and-mortar type pastors of the past. I am more of a people-person type of pastor. Just let me minister to the spiritual needs of my people. I don't know anything about building." Well, not so fast there, Reverend. Let me remind you of a few things, if I may be so bold.

Few if any pastors are builders in the strict bricks-and-mortar sense. That's not how we were trained. But neither were the pastors of the past who shouldered those tasks when needed by previous generations of Christians. You have learned many things during your years in the ministry that were not covered in school. You can learn this and do it well.

Yes, you are meant to be a people-person, a minister for others in the image of Jesus Christ, dedicated to caring for the spiritual needs of your people. But this is not the time to become a Jansenistic dualist. People are souls or spirits that are embodied. We Christians are incarnational. We are a sacramental church. We believe that the physical, the material, the bodily is a vehicle for the spiritual. The physical speaks for and embodies the spiritual. And this portion of the Body of Christ entrusted to your care needs a new physical place in time and space for its worship.

I contend that if done thoughtfully, the building of a new church can be (and moreover, should be) the physical sign or *sacramental* of a Christian community that is the here and now locus of the Body of Christ. Building a new church may in fact be the most sacramental thing you can ever do as a pastor, if you do it right.

Next, let me address a few words to the parishioner asked to serve on a building committee. You may feel honored but are perhaps a bit apprehensive. You may be wondering about time commitments, committee responsibilities, qualifications. Yes, the time required will be significant, but usually it's the busy people who get things done. Committee responsibilities will be explained from the start and clarified as the group solidifies and moves from phase to phase. As an active member of this faith community you *are* qualified. You are a member of the Body of Christ in this place and at this time. You worship and pray with these people. They are you. Plus, you will be given information, education, and formation for the tasks asked of you as a building committee member. Some of those you will find here in this book.

Finally, *Why me?* Because your pastor sees something in you that should be brought to this new church project. It may be your personality, your contacts in the parish, your perspective as a lay person, a special talent, or a past or present involvement. Ask about why you were chosen. In short, your pastor should not, and wisely does not, want to attempt to build this new church alone.

The building of a new church space for a community of Christians is the opportunity to call forth from that faith community deep and lasting elements from within its collective psyche. As a team of pastor and laity who are building a new church with the community, you stand in a place of great influence. Together you have the opportunity to form and shape the spiritual life of this community in a way that may be exceeded only by the influence of the founding pastor and parishioners. And if you are the founding group that is charged with building the community's first permanent worship space, then your influence is more than doubly increased.

To stand in a place of great influence, however, is also to accept great responsibility. If this is truly a physical and a spiritual work, then the pastor and the lay leaders need to be at the center and heart of it. You need to lead the people and lead them well. Together you have come to know this community. With your pastor you have the theological background and prayerful formation necessary for the task. You have been publicly called forth to act officially in the name of this faith community.

In short, if not you, then who? And if you do not do it well, a great opportunity will have been missed. You see, the real task here is for the pastor and the building committee to engage with the parishioners to mutually articulate the faith, the worship history, and the community values unique to these people. Help them clarify, refine, and develop those things. Then let those same values bring forth the community's place of worship. Let the consciously reflected values build the building. I contend that with the right processes, there is a much greater chance that those values will be embodied in the church building that you construct together.

Do some of the processes described in this book take more time and energy? In the long haul, they do not. If done properly from the start (even if it is a bit slower in the beginning), you will not have to spend the time and energy backtracking to fix exclusions, omissions, confusions, and ownership issues at the end. It's like the old oil filter commercial on TV: "You can pay me now; or you can pay me later." X-amount of time and energy spent on these processes up front will definitely be less painful than Y-amount of feuding, defending, and clearing up after construction.

The processes and suggestions described here do not come from a professional. I have never been on a diocesan building commission. I possess no special background in fund-raising. I have no formal training in group process and shared decision making. I have never been an architect or construction manager. I am just a parish priest. What I have learned, I learned the way many people learned their pastoral skills: OJT, on-the-job training.

My specific situation was that I had pastored a growing Catholic faith community for a number of years when the need to build a new church arose. Previously I, as an associate pastor, had seen traditional building programs up close, though none on the scale of an entirely new church (I had seen a school remodeling, and I had led a parish hall expansion and built an office addition). So I asked myself and others many times, why this? and why that way? Frequently I asked myself how I, were I a parishioner, would like to be included, approached, and treated during the building process. I wondered how I would want to be asked and informed about these things. Furthermore, I was blessed in this parish with a very talented and dedicated staff that constantly suggested better ways to go about this task of building a new church. Many of the suggestions that you will read in this book are the resulting answers to those questions.

This book is meant to be an auxiliary guide from one church builder to other church builders. The chapters at times are addressed to the pastor, but the whole volume is intended to include the principal lay leaders of the parish who will work with the pastor in this task of building. All will benefit greatly, I believe, in reading and studying this book individually and together. This small volume is not meant to replace any local diocesan or judicatory documents, guidelines, or processes. It is meant to compliment and supplement them. For those within the Catholic tradition, there is the United States Catholic Conference document *Built of Living Stones: Art, Architecture, and Worship* (2000). Another helpful document with a very practical bent is the Canadian Conference of Catholic Bishops document *Our Place of Worship* (1999).

May God bless your work, and may you be guided by the Carpenter's Son.

*Chapter 2*

# The Roles of the Pastor

Those pastors who have built a new church might tell you that the primary role in this situation is to duck and cover. Although a bit cynical, there is an element of truth to this advice. Building a new church can be fraught with dangers and pitfalls. In large part, the motivation for writing this book was to help steer the pastor and the lay leaders away from those dangers and around the pitfalls.

If not handled in some organized and thoughtful way, building a new church can create tensions and divisions within any congregation. There can be a sense of exclusion and isolation ("That's *his* church, not mine"). Misunderstandings can abound ("I don't see why we needed this"). It can divide a congregation ("I wanted a colonial style. Why did they build Romanesque?"). Communications can break down ("Well, they never asked me about this"). Nevertheless, opinions in all their variety must be sought. Differing ideas need to be aired, alternatives should be explored, and choices should always be explained publicly and clearly. That is what this volume offers, a tested set of processes and procedures that can bridge the pitfalls of building a new church in and for a faith community.

Aware of those dangers, let us forge ahead. As a pastor the roles you will be assuming are divided into three parts. This chapter will outline them and make some specific suggestions about how they could be implemented.

As with any significant project or task, the big question is always where to begin. The critical place to begin is with an understanding of what your roles are in this process. You are the pastor and will continue to be the pastor of a functioning, and probably very busy, Christian faith community. So this new role as a pastor of a parish that is building a church is an additional one. It is a task of major proportions that is being added to your many other pastoral duties. This new role will stretch out over a considerable time period. The tasks involved will require significant amounts of your time.

So the opening question is what are you going to give up in order to accomplish this new job? When a wise pastor who had just completed his own church building project put that question to me, I was a bit shocked. I had never thought in those terms. He insisted that if I was to be successful, it would mean sacrifice. I suppose I thought I would just squeeze building in along with everything else and sacrifice my own time. Isn't that what most of us do with a new church responsibility?

Given the scope, the significance, the investment, and the enduring impact, building a new church is not the kind of thing that can just be squeezed in. That is a mistake easily made, but long regretted. If you as the pastor are not deeply involved in building this new church, if you are not there to balance the theology and insert the liturgical experience, if you do not facilitate the design, then the project will suffer and be less for it. Do you want to live with that? I didn't. It is really a matter of good stewardship, and here the stewardship is of your own time.

But what to give up? Rather than deciding on my own what I would attempt to "not do" in order to have the time and energy for the new church project, I began with a staff gathering to review our individual ministerial responsibilities. This meeting brought the entire staff on board with the task at a very early stage. It gave them ownership in how this project would be accomplished. When it came to me, we listed all the things that I was doing in the parish as a priest and as the pastor. We tried to tag each with the amount of time per week or month that it generally required. Then we listed next to each whether that item required a priest or a pastor to do it. Once these were identified, it was a matter of balancing the impact of priest/pastor withdrawal along with the amount of time recouped. At the same time we did a similar process for the staff members who were to be more intimately involved with the church building process, i.e., the liturgy and music director and the business manager. Along with me these staff members were going to see their workloads expand in the face of this project.

In my own case I wound up cutting back my involvement in the baptismal and marriage preparation programs. We felt this was possible because of a talented adult education and formation staff member, and the impact was lessened as I was still going to celebrate those baptisms and marriages liturgically. As there were some one hundred baptisms and another thirty marriages per year, this yielded a large block of time. There were other duties that I was able to reallocate that produced smaller time blocks. In your case this will vary based on your present involvement and the capacity of your staff. If you don't work out some kind of a reallocation of duties to free you up, you will either not be able to give this job the time and energy it deserves, or you will withdraw, consciously or subconsciously, at some point along the way due to decreased energy (read: burnout). You need to make the time available.

Having addressed the temptation to underestimate the time involved, I would now like to deal with the next and perhaps the greatest temptation: that is, to build your own vision of a church. It is understandable. You have the theology. You have the experience as a priest, a leader of worship, and a pastor. It would be more time efficient. Meetings can involve a minimal number of people. All you need are three: the architect, yourself, and a business/finance person. Right?

Wrong! This is not to be *your* church; it is to be *their* church. Your role as the pastor is to lead and facilitate the building of this new church. It is meant to belong to the entire faith community. No matter how much time you are able to carve out for yourself, no matter how efficient a group of three people might be, do not attempt to build this church alone. This is not the time for you to think "my memorial," or to become a "gang of three." There is more at stake here than simply being efficient or just accomplishing the task. Sure, there are many meetings, much discussion, innumerable decisions to be made, countless choices, and a myriad of details to be tracked. But beyond that there is the core responsibility to facilitate and build the church space *of* this parish, not just *for* this parish. This parish will be here long after you are gone. Help them have the new church that suits *them* best.

Does the Lone Ranger scenario above sound improbable? "No one would really try to build a new church alone." Well, amazingly, they have. There are new churches that have been built by the pastor, the architect, and a couple of friends of the pastor that made up a sort of kitchen cabinet. Sometimes churches have even been built without the few friends. Mostly, they are a disaster. Maybe not a disaster in the physical building that resulted. But certainly it is a disaster because the opportunity for that parish community to have had a more conscious interaction with its beliefs and values and to have those challenged and deepened was missed. Building a new church is a teachable moment in the life of a faith community.

"Ok, I am not the lone builder. Then what should be my role?" In short your principal roles are these: convener, educator, and facilitator. There will be more on these as the roles themselves arise in the later chapters. Your first role is that of convener. A convener is someone who calls together, brings forth, assembles, and empowers others.

Your first convener role, and perhaps one of the most critical to the success of a new church building program, is the determination of a building committee and its structure. You are going to need the help, involvement, and ownership of the parish community as has already been stated. You need to access the history and wisdom that resides in the faith community. You need to have a vehicle for the two-way flow of ideas and information. This vehicle needs to be clear to all and understood by the whole parish.

To not create a formal committee structure is to risk the appearance (or the reality) that the new church is the project of a few, and not of the whole community. Unknown or misunderstood methods of input and decision making have the potential to undermine the ownership and credibility factors. Unclear lines of communication can lead people to think that the last speaker might be the determiner of an outcome. Other than trying to run the whole new church project by yourself, the next temptation is to have an informal group of advisers or a casual committee. Structure is important, and the structure needs to be clear and well publicized. Along with clear structures is the need for accountability, accountability to the people of the parish through the interaction of the building committee with the ordinary structures of the parish (parish council, finance council, and other parish committees).

There are many models available for a building committee structure. I strongly suggest you develop one that is solely dedicated to the new church project. Do not attempt to use the existing structure of the parish council and/or the parish finance committee. They will either be overwhelmed by both the new and the old, or they will choose one over the other. Besides, you need these existing bodies to continue the ongoing work of the parish. Everyday tasks, planning, decisions, and ordinary financial needs will continue on a regular basis while the new church is in process. Make sure, though, that the existing structures (parish council, finance committee, liturgy, environment, grounds, etc.) stay in communication with the new church building committee structure that you create. If these standing committees are adequately staffed with a number of parishioners, then you should consider recommending that they or you select one member from each to be on the various subcommittees that are mentioned below (e.g., liturgy, finance, parish newsletter/bulletin editor, grounds). If you do not take one member from each as a committee or subcommittee member for the building committee structure, then designate building committee people to be liaisons between the parallel structures. Just make sure the standing committees of the parish do not feel left out and that they know what is going on with the new church. As the building project develops, make sure they are interacting in a consultative way with the building committees.

For our church building committee structure, we began with a central *steering committee* independent of, but communicating with, the parish council and finance committee. This committee was selected after consultation with staff members, and with a view to broad representation of ages and parish involvements. Although not strictly representative in a demographic or political sense, the steering committee members were chosen with a view to the extent of their contacts with other parishioners, both individuals and groups, formal and informal. In addition to the pastor, the steering committee membership included the parish liturgy and music director and the parish business and finance manager. They are essential in my judgment to a project of this nature. Subcommittees were chaired by steering committee members and added other parishioners with talents and/or interests specific to that subcommittee's task, seeking some representation from among the standing committees of the parish. The subcommittees became involved at various points as the project unfolded.

The subcommittees that we used were the following. *Communications* saw to the general and specific information being delivered to the parishioners through various means (bulletin, newsletter, web site, special bulletin inserts, celebration events, and dedication booklets). *Fund-raising* worked on the actual capital campaign and saw to the case statements, appeal letters, thank-you notes, advance, and special gifts. *Furnishings* undertook the work of coordinating the interior elements such as pews, altar, ambo, celebrant's chair, baptistry, ambry, kneelers, sanctuary and vestibule seating. *Artwork* was reserved for the specially commissioned pieces such as statuary, paintings, stained or etched glass windows, and liturgical items, along with the selection, adaptation, and transfer of existing treasured objects from the present to the future church. *Landscaping* was concerned with planting coordination, watering systems, outdoor art (statuary, fountains, etc.), prayer garden, courtyard, and the cornerstone. (See appendix 1, http://www.litpress.org/PDFs/new_church/appendix1.pdf, for a sample organizational chart.)

The only committee that is absolutely dependent on your presence for input and direction all the time is the steering committee. You do not need to be a permanent working member of all the subcommittees. You may come and go as their work requires your presence. For example, you can provide basic information when they begin their tasks, occasionally drop by for encouragement and questions, and facilitate should they get stuck. This will usually prove to be sufficient. You have delegated them to the task; let them do it. If, however, you have strong feelings about a particular area or item (e.g., the placement of the baptistry, devotional space, statuary, or the like), then it is important to state that up front and to be involved in the subcommittee deliberations on that issue rather than doing a surprise overruling after the subcommittee work is complete. Otherwise you will lose leadership credibility and the parishioners involved in the subcommittees may lose ownership for their subcommittee work.

The educator role that you bring to the steering committee is a familiarity with liturgical documents (the Second Vatican Council, curial, national, and diocesan), insofar as they pertain to the building of a new church. You do not have to be an expert in this. You may be able to call on your diocesan director of liturgy for help in this regard, or you may want an outside liturgical consultant. Whatever you do, you do need to be familiar with the documents. So brush up and do some studying.

In addition it will be a great help if you have some knowledge about the development of church buildings through the centuries. An acquaintance with the architectural elements of a church building will go a long way in discovering how to translate a theme into a structure (see chap. 12). The ability to be able to read a blueprint will allow you to understand the building as it develops (ask your architect for help with the basics). If nothing else you should prepare yourself by viewing photographs of churches, past and present, as well as local, national, and international examples. No one can afford today to build a Notre Dame of Paris or a Duomo in Milan, but you can learn from them and possibly incorporate some of their ecclesial elements into today's structures.

Finally, you will assume the role of facilitator. The task here is to draw others into the process. The undertaking for you and your steering committee is to expand participation and input through various forms and forums such as surveys, polls, town-hall meetings, focus groups, and the like. The goal is to give the broadest spectrum of the parish real participation in and ownership of the building of this new church. This is how they will come to truly believe that this is their church, that they were heard, and that this church is a genuine fit for them. These efforts will go a long way to lower tensions and diffuse conflicts.

The facilitator role may be the one that tries your patience the most. The temptation here will be to just decide it yourself, whatever it is. Resist! Some of the best ideas may come from the most unlikely places. It will take more time than deciding it yourself or in the steering committee, but this is the price of empowering your people as they come to take hold of their own ecclesiology. It will pay great dividends in the long run, far beyond the construction of a building.

# Chapter 3

# Assessing the Need

There are many ways to do a needs assessment. In fact, there are professionals who can lead the parish through an expert process. These consultants have their place and function to perform. I would strongly recommend these specially skilled people if you are faced with building a church amid any special or difficult circumstances. Some possible examples would include but not be limited to the following:

- If the pastor is brand new to the parish, and he is under pressure to build immediately without the time to get to know the community and knowledgeably assess its needs

- If this is a new parish, split off from one or more existing parishes, and has not settled into its own identity yet

- If the parish has experienced a recent crisis (sexual abuse scandal, prior pastor leaving the priesthood, discovery of financial irregularities, and such) that has shaken its identity and confidence

If the parish has experienced one of these situations, then I think it is wise to use the help of professionals to discover if this is the time to move forward with a new church building. There are some circumstances within a faith community that preclude undertaking the task of building a new church. It may not be the right time, but you need skilled folks to help you arrive at that conclusion.

Barring these and other difficult circumstances, you and the steering committee can conduct your own needs assessment. Your needs assessment should include demographics, finances, and structural questions. Let's begin with the demographics, the numbers in your locale that you will need to assess your future growth. All numbers should count individuals, not registered families or households. If your parish census is computerized, run an individual count. If not, the average household size is available on the U.S. Census web site at State and County Quick Facts, under "Persons per Household." In the United States the overall size is 2.6 persons per household as of 2006. But check your state and county for a more localized estimate.

You have to begin with an accurate count of what your present church or worship space holds. You want to know what a full church means. Don't guess. Don't estimate. Don't eyeball it. Get real numbers. If your church has Masses that are already full, do actual head counts. Divide the church into segments and have the ushers count heads during the collection/offertory time. If you have people standing at Mass, be sure it is because there is no more room in the pews. If your pews are of uniform length, then gather some people and find out how many fit in one when it is full, both spread-out-relaxed full and squeezed-in-Christmas full.

Next, begin to build a Mass attendance database if you don't already have one. Have the ushers do accurate head counts at every Mass for a month. That will give you an average. If you do this, say in September, November, and February you will have a good handle on your attendance. Be sure they note the numbers that are standing, sitting in extra chairs that are set up in the vestibule, or are seated in a cry room without an infant. It will be helpful if you add head counts for holy days, Christmas, and Easter. You might be able to redistribute some of that space by varying the times of the services once you know the patterns. This could alleviate some of your more extreme crowding problems. Continue to do regular head counts in your database. This will be a good verification of growth rates. All the better if you have averages from past years or have the time to accumulate them.

Your next step is to take the database of average weekly attendance and divide it by your total registered parish population, assuming that you have purged your membership list for those who have moved, joined other parishes, etc. This will give you the percentage of attendance for your area. By the way, the average weekly attendance at Sunday Mass for Roman Catholics in the United States in 2006 was somewhere between 34 and 38 percent. Depressing as that may be, just remember that this is one of the highest in the Western world. Much of Europe, including Italy, is in the 10 percent or below range.

Now you want to determine the percentage of Catholics in the general population of your area. Your diocese may have statistics on the Catholic population in the area or diocese that they can share with you. If not, then see if there is an area planning council. Frequently these are organized by metropolitan, county, or regional areas. They are a wonderful source of statistical information not only for this question but also for future growth. What you want is the total population within your parish boundaries. Then you can divide the number of your registered Catholics of the parish by the total population. That will give you the percentage of Catholics within the population.

If there is no accessible information from the diocese or a regional council, then you still can roughly determine the percentage for your locale. Find out the census tracks that make up your parish (often an election office can be helpful). You may have to split census tracks to match the parish boundaries. Try to do so proportionally. Then divide your number of parishioners into the matching area census track population. Again, what you are looking for here is a rough percentage to work with for future growth.

Next, see if your metropolitan/county area planning council (or sometimes school districts) can provide you with growth projections. Most municipal governments generate this information. What you want are the growth projections for your area for the next five, ten, and twenty years. If you can access past growth projections, say from five and ten years ago, then compare them to the actual growth to see how accurate the projections have been. You may not need to factor in this percentage of overage/underage. Ideally the demographers have gotten better with time and have factored it in already. Find out if there is a significant percentage difference between the projected and the actual if you can.

Now the steering committee is ready to crunch some numbers, as they say. Take the projected growth number for each time segment (five, ten, twenty years), multiply that by the percentage of Catholics in the area, and multiply that result by the percentage of Mass attendance. This should give you a good idea of the number of people attending Mass that will need to be accommodated on any given weekend in the future. Now divide that number by the number of Mass celebrations that are realistic in light of available priests. The typical priest can celebrate three Masses of obligation on a weekend over and above any weekend funerals and weddings.

Here's an example. Let's say that St. Cunegunda Parish now has 6,000 registered parishioners (adults and children). Actual head counts over a number of months or years indicate an average weekend Mass attendance of 2,340, producing an attendance percentage of 39 percent $(2,340 \div 6,000 = .39 \times 100 = 39\%)$. Two of the three present weekend Masses are crowded, requiring additional chairs along the aisles and in the vestibule plus some standing. There is only one priest with no expectation of more in the foreseeable future.

The population of the area according to the last census (or its midterm projections) was 28,500 $(6,000 \div 28,500 = .2105 \times 100 = 21.05\%)$. The rough percentage of registered Catholics in the St. Cunegunda area relative to the population is 21.05.

The planning data of the regional council here projects that the growth in this area over the next twenty years will be 29 percent. So in twenty years the area population should be 36,765 $(28,500 \times 1.29 = 36,765)$. The Catholic share of that ought to be 7,739 $(36,765 \times .2105 = 7,739)$ or an increase of 1,739 people $(7,739 - 6,000 = 1,739)$.

So in twenty years St. Cunegunda's will have around 7,739 Catholics. But we know from our collected database that the average percentage of attendance at weekend Masses is 39 percent of the registered parishioners. So in twenty years this parish will need to accommodate 3,018 $(7,739 \times .39 = 3,018)$ people in whatever number of Masses are celebrated—that is, an additional 678 $(3,018 - 2,340 = 678)$ Mass-attending parishioners.

Here is where you want to return to your Mass attendance database and calculate your Mass distribution numbers. As you well know, unless your parish is most unusual, people do not evenly distribute themselves over a Mass schedule. You need to know on average what percentage of the total weekend Mass attendance is represented at any given Mass. You can do this by taking your average attendance at a Mass and divide it by the total weekend attendance. If, for example, the 10:00 a.m. Mass has an average attendance of 850 individuals and the total weekend attendance is 2,340, then this Mass has a 36.32 percent distribution of the weekend Mass attendance $([850 \div 2,340] \times 100 = 36.32\%)$.

Repeat this formula for each Mass to find the distribution percentages. Next take your twenty-year future Mass attendance and apply the distribution percentage to estimate future Mass distribution. In our example St. Cunegunda Parish will have 3,018 Mass-attending Catholics in twenty years; and, assuming the same number of weekend obligation Masses at approximately the same times, then the 10:00 a.m. (mid-morning) Mass will need to accommodate 1,096 people (3,018 × .3632 = 1,096). (See appendix 2, http://www.litpress.org/PDFs/new_church/appendix2.pdf, for a list of these demographic formulae.)

Let me close this section on demographics with a couple of last thoughts. I would suggest you run all the above calculations for the ten-year projected population numbers as well as the twenty-year projections. Furthermore, if the growth in the area is of a different ethnic population, be sure to adjust your projections upward or downward accordingly, but be conservative. You may want to share the results with the parishioners to give them an idea of the growth that has already occurred in the past five (or even ten) years. This will anchor the crowding issue in some hard data. Also, sharing with the parishioners the five- and ten-year projections of future growth will let them know some of the hard facts about the possible need to build anew. You may want to share this information in the parish bulletin or newsletter, and if you believe that it is warranted, in a Sunday homily. (A sample homily outline is found in appendix 3.1, http://www.litpress.org/PDFs/new_church/appendix3.pdf.)

Next let's take up the financials. Even before estimating what you might be able to raise in a new church building campaign (best done by professional fund-raisers), what excess funds is the parish now generating over and above ordinary operation expenses? What surplus revenues are being put on deposit in savings now? If you are currently paying down a past debt, when will it end? Will the past debt revenues continue to flow into the parish as ordinary income that can be directed to a savings account for the new church building once the old debt is paid off? Or once the old debt is paid will that money cease?

Some dioceses require a certain percentage of the estimated cost of a building project to be secured in advance of any loans. This is usually a combination of cash on hand and pledges of future donations. Be sure to check early on with the diocesan finance office what the loan policy is for new church buildings. Plans for the new church may need to be postponed until the parish builds up a financial reserve even before launching a formal building campaign.

Let me state and restate that any and all monies that are saved in advance of the formal building campaign will generate a huge momentum in the fund drive. Monies set aside for the new church during the planning process and before the capital campaign begins are pure gold.

In our building situation we were able to accumulate a surplus (some 20 percent of the final building costs) from ordinary income that the parishioners knew was being earmarked for future capital needs.

Presently, the steering committee needs to sit down and undertake a realistic analysis of the parish finances. With a sharp pencil and a critical eye, take a hard look at the present financial picture to see if this is the time to begin this building process. It is not a good idea to cripple the many ministries and programs of the parish now or in the future with a burdensome debt. What amount can be put aside in savings out of the current operating revenue? What has been the parish's track record of saving or of debt repayment?

At this very early and hazy stage of estimating project costs, find out what recently built churches of a similar size in the area have cost (usually stated in dollars per square foot). Be sure to add to the building cost (if not included in the quoted price) the cost of the architects (usually a percentage of the building's cost), furnishings (often a separate budget), artwork (again, often a separate budget), and so on. Then be sure to add any appropriate diocesan assessments (*cathedradicum*) on revenue raised to build the new church and pay down its debt. In my diocese this adds almost 10 percent to project costs unless the money is already deposited and the assessment already paid. The point here is not to be blindsided by unanticipated cost factors before the total project cost is understood (more on total project costs in chap. 14). Later in the process you will need to create financial cash flows during construction and repayment spreadsheets based on the length of the loan (see chap. 18).

This early, albeit rough, financial work gives you a preliminary idea of whether it is possible to go ahead. It also enlightens all as to what will be needed from the fund-raising campaign. After the capital campaign is completed, a more specific discussion should be held on these same topics. The probable revenue or capital income will be known at that point.

Now let's turn to a key structural question. Should there be an expansion of the present church facility, or the building of an entirely new one? This question has to be resolved early on so that all the options are on the table for a decision. It will be hard to rally universal support if a portion of the parish believes that an alternative solution to church crowding at Mass was not addressed.

This is a highly individualized issue. It depends on so many factors indigenous to the local community and situation. These are important questions that the steering committee should formally and seriously address. All of us have seen parishes build in the wrong place and/or at the wrong time.

Questions like these should be given adequate discussion: Do we have adequate land (acreage) at this location? Remember, a larger capacity church will require more parking space. Is more contiguous land available for purchase at a reasonable price? Do we have the space to build the size of facility we should for the future (at least twenty years)? Is the present location of the parish adequate and appropriate for the probable future growth? Is the parish in the right place or will it have to be relocated in the future? How does a relocation based on future growth patterns impact this building project? Is this the time to address the question of relocation? Future diocesan plans are important, so be sure to check with any diocesan planning office.

Once the present location is settled, the steering committee should address the question of expanding the present church or building a new one. You will need the services of a structural engineer. There are two main questions here. First, is the present church building worth adding onto? And second, is the present church architecturally adaptable to an addition?

The first question about worthiness involves the physical condition of the present church (foundation, structural integrity, roof, plumbing, electrical, fire suppression, heating and air-conditioning systems). How much work and how expensive will it be to bring the building up to present code requirements? Upgrading work on older buildings can be expensive. There is no point in adding onto a building that is beyond its serviceable lifetime. Remember also that in an addition the use of the building (or parts of it) will be lost while work is underway. What space will be used for Mass during this renovation?

The second question is about architectural and aesthetic values. Almost any sound building can be added onto. But what will it look like? Will it be a fitting structure for the celebration of the sacred mysteries? The people are owed a certain element of beauty beyond function. Will there be some support beam that divides the old space from the new? Will there be different ceiling heights? Uneven floor transitions? Will the body of the church be a singular, unified space? What will the sight lines for the altar be like? What will the acoustical considerations be in this newly created space? An architect may need to be consulted on some of these questions. Almost anything can be built with enough money. The question here is, will it be a fitting and worthy place for worship?

Having addressed some of the fundamental direction questions (population and demographics, preliminary issues of funding and finance, and basic structural options of expansion or new construction), we are ready to move on.

## Chapter 4

# Parishioner Communications

In chapter 2 I outlined three basic roles for the pastor: convener, educator, facilitator. In addition to convening the steering committee and the various subcommittees, the entire parish needs to be convened. The parishioners need to be brought together so that everyone can hear what is said about a new church. And the parishioners need to be made aware of the fruit of the committee's work. So in this chapter I want to address the general issue of communications—the steering committee to the parishioners and the parishioners back to the committee.

Let me begin by saying that there is no such thing as too much communication with the parish during the process of building a new church. It is the old saw: say what you are going to say, say it, say what you have said, and then say it again. It takes time and repetition for any complex message to sink into the collective consciousness of the parish community. Even though you may think you have overdone it, you have to remember that you are living with these ideas and concerns on a daily basis. The parish needs to hear them, hear them clearly, and hear them repeatedly.

Communication is a two-way street. Not only do they need to hear you, you need to be able to hear the people. And you need to hear all of the people, not just those who may be close to you or on the committees. There is a lot of wisdom out there, a lot of lived faith experience, and a lot of energy. So make sure you have multiple ways to receive feedback. Make sure everyone on the committee realizes that a key component of their job is to listen to their fellow parishioners and to gather information as well as to dispense it.

And be sure to hear what people are really saying, not just the words, but the ideas behind them. I'll give you a wonderful example. When we were in an early phase of the design development, and we had put out a model for people to react to, I noticed that I was getting a number of questions from older female parishioners about whether there would be a choir loft. None of them were in the choir and this parish had never had a choir loft, so I wondered what was behind this issue. Finally, after the umpteenth inquiry about a choir loft, I asked the questioner why she was asking about a choir loft as she did not belong to the choir. She said that being older now and somewhat short in stature, she was hoping a choir loft would help her see the altar area rather than the backs of other people in a crowded church. Ta-da! The real question was one of visibility and line of sight. I explained to her that there would be a gentle slope to the floor and that the altar would be elevated a couple of steps. She was delighted. Shorter folks would have a good line of sight. No need for a choir loft. So be sure to inquire enough to find out the real issue that underlies the question.

Looking at some of the forms of communication available in this situation, most of them are familiar to you and in use already. The summary here is a reminder to use them, and vary them throughout these upcoming processes. They each have their own advantages and their own audiences. I have divided them into two basic formats: the spoken word and the written word.

Spoken communications with the parish for our purposes include: town-hall meetings (large group meetings); focus groups (small group meetings); straw polls (large group information session with a voted response); homilies (important information and educational matters within the context of the Sunday Mass). Of course there is the casual conversation any member of the steering committee may have with one or more parishioners in an informal way. These can be great ways to see how effective the broader communications are and what may need further explanation and reinforcing. Be sure the steering committee is always testing its effectiveness.

In our building project we used the town-hall format to bring to-gether a large number of parishioners (e.g., a 7:00 to 9:00 p.m. meet-ing in the parish hall). This type of meeting is good for disseminating important information, study results, big ideas, and their details. A question-and-answer portion is critical to allow for feedback, further clarifications, understanding, and acceptance. Be sure to include it.

Our first use of the town-hall format was to present the results of the steering committee's needs assessment (the numbers and the formula results) and to determine the answer to the question of "expand the old versus build the new." Such a critical question as old versus new required us to hold more than a single meeting to be sure to reach the maximum number of parishioners. The steering committee explained our current church capacity, priest limitations for the future (ten and twenty years) in the diocese, and the projected number of attending Catholics in the future. We were already very crowded in our existing church, so this was not a hard sell. The main question was expansion of the old church or construction of a new one. Here we brought in a structural engineer to clarify the limitations of the present building. All the staff were present at each of these town-hall meetings to show the importance of and support for this decision. After the presentations, questions were fielded from the floor by me, the committee, and the engineer. The evening ended with a vote of acceptance.

Although the decision itself was pretty obvious once we had the demographic data and the engineer's report, I felt it was important for this critical decision to be faced by the parish at large. The material, although somewhat complex, was laid out item by item for the people present in each meeting. With the parish coming to the same conclusion as the steering committee that had assembled the data and received the original engineer's report, a strong level of community consensus was achieved. No storming ahead by a pastor or a committee without information and group support. No smoke-filled backroom decisions. All clear and out in the open. It was a classic case of spending the time up front making our case to avoid spending our time later defending the decision.

A focus group is a gathering of a relatively small group of people selected to match an age, an area, or an opinion demographic (i.e., a small group representative of the large group or whole). This can be used to gain insight into matters of taste, opinion, or preference. They can be helpful with discretional choices (e.g., textures, colors, surfaces, styles) in a most general way. Let me stress those last words, *in a general way*. Designs have to possess an integrity and a wholeness. They usually suffer when cooked up by too many hands. Remember that a camel was a horse designed by a focus group! In short, broad directions can be gained here but not specific details. For example, should the new

church be in the cluster style (connected and accessible to other buildings) or in the campus style (free-standing and spread out)? What are
the treasured objects of the existing church that should be reclaimed
for the new church?

A straw poll is a technique in which you bring a fairly simple question to the parishioners in a large group. The choice must be clearly
defined. It must be able to be explained in a short time. It does not
allow for questions or discussion. That has to have already occurred
at another time and in another format. It is a way to get a quick directional choice out of a large group of parishioners. We did a number of
straw polls with the parish. These were done at the weekend Masses,
usually at the time of the announcements (but we alerted to the coming poll earlier in the Mass, perhaps at the beginning of the homily).
The method was a vote by raising hands that were tallied by a number
of counters. If the counts were close (versus overwhelmingly one way
or the other) we would take that topic to a future town-hall meeting
for further exploration.

The pulpit is a very powerful communication tool. It was used
throughout the building process almost exclusively for education and
very important information. In fact, early on in the process, and after
assessing the need, a Sunday homily was dedicated to the process that
we were entering as a parish. This was done for two reasons: to let the
people know that the building process would be a consultative one in
which they were expected to be involved (to be educated before being
consulted), and to apprise them that there would be many diocesan steps
and procedures that we would be required to take as a parish before per-
mission to build would be given. (See appendix 3.2, http://www.litpress
.org/PDFs/new_church/appendix3.pdf, for a sample homily outline.)

Within the context of the lectionary cycle of readings, the pulpit
came into play for a number of educational presentations to inform and
educate the parishioners about such things as the liturgical documents,
architectural histories, the place of art and music, the spiritual renewal
of a new church, and so forth. At times consultants were brought in for
a topic, but most educational offerings were presented by the pastor
and staff. Educational content was also addressed in adult educational
offerings throughout the building process. If the entire staff feels a
part of this project, they can integrate it into many places of parish
life within their own programs.

One last thought on the spoken communications: use the regular
meetings of parish groups (altar society, mothers' group, Holy Name

Society, Knights of Columbus, senior citizens' group, etc.) to drop in, make brief informational presentations, field questions. Then send the members out as newly minted informational delegates for the new church building.

Now let us turn to written communications with the parish. For our purposes here this will include the bulletin (for regular, ongoing information), bulletin inserts (for longer, more detailed pieces along with graphics), the parish newsletter (for regular updates as well as special items; remember that when mailed out, this reaches those not at a particular weekend Mass for the bulletin), a new church building newsletter (dedicated solely to the new church building project), and special publications. Those are the types of printed communications that we used. There are undoubtedly other formats. Use them, especially if they are already familiar to your parishioners. Again, there is no such thing as too much communication. And don't forget to put any and all of this on your parish web site.

Every parish has a weekly bulletin. This reaches the parishioners who attend Mass so they are informed about the events of the week. Some parishes even mail a monthly bulletin that covers events for the coming month to be sure it reaches all the registered households. Consider making a special section of the bulletin (weekly and mailed version) for the new church building news. Give it a recognizable and catchy title. Call people's attention to it frequently. By its nature this vehicle will be for brief and simple informational updates: e.g., pictures of the steering committee, abbreviated minutes of their meetings, information as it is gathered, results of straw polls, etc.

Bulletin inserts are useful for longer and more detailed pieces of information. They are simply a printed page inserted into the bulletin itself. This helps with longer, written pieces without crowding out the ongoing, regular business of the parish. This is great when you have lots of pictures of the building under construction (print in color if you can) to share with parishioners. Inserts also can be used for a question-and-answer page or items that the steering committee is hearing along the way and wants to address or clarify.

Parish newsletters need to be well presented in their layout and graphics. The key to readability is that they provide information that the bulletin does not. The danger here is that a parish newsletter can begin to look like a longer bulletin. Our rule of thumb was that the newsletter was primarily for educational material rather than announcements. Sure, we had a calendar and reported on upcoming and recent events, but we always tried for a content-related article or two on some topic of educational significance.

A format that falls between a full-blown newsletter dedicated to the new church is the inserted page for the new church building in the regular parish newsletter. This is always an option, and one that can lead up to the full new church building newsletter as the project gains momentum. In either format, newsletters are the place to repeat and expand educational articles that are related to the new church. You have the space and the vehicle for the whole parish community.

Special publications can include items like a parish history that can be included in a pictorial directory, a possible groundbreaking booklet or program, the dedication booklet, the dedication program, and the like. There will be more on these later. The basic principle in this whole communications chapter is to use any and all forms that you now have in the parish along with creating some new ones to spread and keep the information and enthusiasm before as many of the parishioners as possible. A solid foundation of good and frequent communication will pay dividends in the coming stages of the building process.

A special word here before moving on to the chapters on the selection of architects and fund-raisers. A good case can be made that if your parish has never done any strategic planning (i.e., broad based, coordinated ministry planning, mission statement processes or visioning), you may want to glance at chapter 7 next. Serious consideration should be given to implementing some form of professionally led strategic planning *before* moving into the architect and fund-raiser selection processes. On the other hand if you have done such planning fairly recently and just some updating is needed, you can move on to architect selection.

## Chapter 5

# Selecting an Architect

This chapter on hiring an architect and the next on employing a fund-raising firm, may be as important to the outcome of the new church as is the selection of the actual contractor who will construct the building. So as the pastor you would do well to *fully* involve the steering committee in these decisions.

It would be important to begin with what the parameters are. Check to see what the local diocesan guidelines may be for the selection of an architect. Some dioceses have prequalified lists of architects and ways to add others to that list. Talk to local pastors who have built recently to discover their experience with particular architects.

The relationship between the architect and the client is multi-faceted. The architect is part technician who oversees the physical construction of the building, along with the engineers (civil, structural, mechanical, electrical, and acoustical), and guides you through building codes, inspections, and safety factors. But the architect is also an artist who gives form and shape to the dreams and desires of a faith community. The architect is charged with being an inspector general and police officer to see that the contractor does what the plans and specifications call for. And still, the architect is like a conductor who is able to listen to the many soundtracks laid down by the community in town-hall meetings and surveys, and can blend and process them into a coherent symphony of sound. The architect produces the broad and sweeping strokes of the master plan's sketches; that same architect then develops excruciatingly detailed pages of how this all goes together. The

architect is charged with melding those dreams for worship and celebration to the materials of earth and structures of people. Remember,
though, the architect works for you, and not vice versa.

To make the best selection I strongly advise that each serious candi-
date for the job of architect is interviewed in person. This will require
the development of a set of criteria for selection. It would be wise for
the steering committee to work this out while preparing the selection
and interview process.

The first step is to assemble a list of architects. If there is not a
diocesan list, then inquire about architects among pastors of recent
building projects both within your denomination and outside it. You
might also let the parishioners know so that they may suggest names
of architects. (This seeking the input from parishioners regarding specific services is a wise and prudent move from this stage on through
contractors, subcontractors, vendors, suppliers, etc. But be sure that
all services and suppliers go through the proper chain of command and
are under the supervision of the proper professional, i.e., no sideline or
nighttime electricians who are not licensed, bonded, and under contract
to the general contractor.)

Next, the potential architects should be contacted by letter appris-
ing them of your intentions and your project, and soliciting from them
their interest, qualifications, references, and availability within your
time frame. They should respond with this information including a
profile of their firm, its staff, company structure, and their previous
projects of a similar nature. Usually a deadline for response is included
in the initial correspondence. Be sure to acknowledge the receipt of
their reply and let them know that you will be contacting them in the
near future as you sort through the architectural candidates who have
applied and the ones with which you want to pursue an interview.

Meanwhile the homework begins here. The responses of each architectural firm need to be reviewed. Check their references for clients
with similar projects. They may send a list of all their recent projects.
The only items of interest are churches, not shopping malls or office
buildings. Talk directly to the pastors of these church buildings and to
their building committee people (perhaps pastor to pastor and steering committee member to committee member). Listen more than you
talk. Listen to what they say, and what they don't say. Remember to
factor in that the parties giving references chose these architects to
build their buildings, so they are naturally going to commend them to
some degree. Anything less is a red flag.

"What questions should we ask?" Here is where a list of criteria comes in. These criteria form part of the basis of evaluation while you are checking the architects' references of previous projects. These are the things to listen for in phone interviews with pastors and committee members who worked with the architect on previous projects.

I suggest that the steering committee begins with a criteria discussion so that a set of items, mutually understood and accepted, can be decided on to form the interview questions with architects. An evaluation form based on those criteria should allow fair comparison of various architects.

Let's begin with the items that will form the criteria used during an interview. Beyond the basic requirements of licensing, insurance, bonding, availability, etc., and the necessary issue of fees (usually a percentage of the basic cost of the building itself), pay schedules, and contracts (some dioceses have their own format), I would suggest that the following be addressed.

Pay very close attention to how the actual working architects and the related professions present at the interview interact and respond to questions. This seems so simple and obvious you must think it is foolish. It is not. A long-term relationship will result from this hiring. Ask yourselves, "Can we work with these people? Do we like them?" One danger is that a senior partner or two may attempt to do the interview. They may be very good, but they may not be the actual working architects who will be assigned to the project. They may be great listeners, facilitators, leaders, and so on, but if they are not going to be the actual people attending all the meetings with the steering committee, listening to the parishioners at town-hall meetings, and such, then you have not learned much. Make sure you understand the architect's office structure and that you are interviewing the right parties.

Now ask this working team of architects (versus the whole firm) what their track record is. How many churches of your size have they done? How many in the past ten years? How many were on time, and if not, why? How many were on budget, and if not, why? If your church is much larger or much smaller than what they have done in the past, how do they anticipate dealing with that difference?

A technical question often asked in requests for interest or during interviews is how many change orders there were on previous projects. (A change order is an alteration in the construction documents after they have been drawn, approved, finalized, and bid. They can be the result of an omission in the original plans, a requested change or addition by the owner, etc.). Unless you ask many more questions to find out what, when, where, and why, I have found that just the number of change orders tells you very little. Change orders are frequently bundled together, so there may be only three, four, or five, but they may contain multiple items for tens of thousands of dollars. Dollar amounts, especially increases in costs to the construction, can tell you something. But again you have to know more. The clients may have asked for something to be added that they did not think of during the original design phase. And there actually can be change orders that reduce the cost of construction, but these usually present themselves during the value engineering stage (more on that phase in chap. 14).

Ask in some detail what processes they plan to use in helping your parish develop its master plan. Discover who and how many of their staff will be involved. Have them state what they have learned doing these processes for other parishes and churches; what works well and what does not? Will they just listen to the parish's needs or will they elicit the parishioners' hopes and dreams so that they can come to know the people?

An aside: I was blessed with some wonderful architects who had at least one member from their working team attend *every* town-hall meeting, question-and-answer session, and survey meeting that we held. They sat in the back. They rarely spoke unless called upon to answer a question. But they took copious notes and one of them almost constantly sketched ideas that she heard. By the time pen went to paper, these architects knew the people and the community pretty well.

That leads to the question of how well they listen. This is critical. Are they open to hearing? Open to teaching? Are they able to draw in and engage? How do they treat the steering committee members as they ask questions and engage with them (they will be doing this with many parishioners too)? Are they good at it? Are they "user friendly," to use a well-worn phrase? They must be able to listen, revise, present, listen some more, revise again, present again, listen, revise, present. They must be able to do this in a cycle of parish to architect to steering committee to parish to architect.

Explore their experience and comfort levels with the aesthetics-creativity-style question. If the desired style of church is already known, be sure the architects are familiar with that style (e.g., your neighborhood is done in a Spanish mission style, and your architect has only done contemporary modern churches). Beyond neighborhood code and style restrictions, I would hope that you would seek an architect with a broad range of styles and abilities. It gives you a larger field within which to work as you discover what fits the needs and wants of the people.

Finally, there is what we came to call the X-factor. This is the intangible, gut feeling, "singing from same page" factor. Reread the paragraph above about the relationship between the architect and the client, about all that the architects have to be—technician, artist, inspector, police officer, conductor, teacher, and listener. It is a lot to ask of anyone, architect or parish. It is like a marriage where the partners mutually choose each other. After all the other criteria are met, "they just seem like the folks for us." It is that graced moment that allows architects and parish communities to come together to create a church that does not belong to the architects, the pastor, or the steering community, but truly belongs to the people.

You will find a sample architect interview form in appendix 4 (http://www.litpress.org/PDFs/new_church/appendix4.pdf). Our steering committee developed this together to assure our mutual understanding and agreement on the criteria. We used it with each architectural firm that we interviewed. It is very important that the whole committee be present for every interview, sometimes doing two or three in the same session (some would say do them all on the same day if possible). We used a ten-point scoring system (10 high and 1 low) throughout all categories so the results can be weighted yet still compared among various interviews. A suggested compilation form is found in appendix 5 (http://www.litpress.org/PDFs/new_church/appendix5.pdf) for the comparison of results from different architectural firms.

It is a good idea to plan the interview format in some detail. You want it to go smoothly, and you want to be able to listen closely. This will be easier if you have decided which member is going to ask which question and its follow-ups. Divide the interview among various members to assure that you get your criteria covered. Have each member score all categories on their own individual form either as the interview is occurring or immediately thereafter. Only after all candidates have been interviewed should you convene to review and compare scores. These numeric scores are less absolute numbers than they are more ways of initiating the discussion necessary to arrive at a decision.

Inform the architectural firms to be interviewed how long they are expected to be present for the interview, how long for questions and answers, what you are looking for, and what you want to know about them. If their presentation is a hard sell and reflects that they did not pay attention to those directives, then it is likely they will not pay attention to other things you want in your building project. Fortunately, this rarely happens these days.

Remember throughout, the selection of an architectural firm and an architect is among the most important decisions that will be made. Take your time. Check references. Interview their previous clients. Ask around. Visit their finished buildings. Be critical in the interviews. Be sure you have a match, a marriage, if you will, between you, the architect, and the parish. And remember, your part in this marriage with the architect (and engineers, contractors, etc.) is to come to all meetings on time and prepared, to respond promptly to their requests, to make decisions, and to pay for services in a timely manner. Those things will keep the relationship moving along smoothly and expeditiously for everyone. And as in a good marriage, clear communication and a mechanism for mutual accountability should be established from the outset and reviewed frequently.

*Chapter 6*

# Selecting a Fund-Raiser

If you have been in pastoral ministry for more than ten years, you have undoubtedly encountered a capital fund-raising campaign either in a parish or in the diocese. These capital campaigns are guided and run by campaign consultants.

Capital campaign consultants or fund-raisers are usually responsible first for a feasibility study. This is a survey to determine, through various instruments, what is the financial potential of a capital campaign in this locale. In other words, how much money can be raised and how should you proceed? A principal element of this study is the one-on-one interview, either in person, in focus groups, or at times by telephone. The number of such contacts is in part determined by the size of the parish. The larger the sample the more accurate the estimated amount will be. Personal contacts are more helpful and telling than a mailed survey. Be sure to tie down the number of contacts a firm intends to conduct for the feasibility study and their methods. In fact, you may want to review their questions for such interviews to get a feel for what they are asking and why. In addition, you may instruct the consulting firm to mail a survey to each household. You will be giving everyone an opportunity to participate, even though only around 10 percent will typically respond. Hence this may be a waste of money. This becomes your call depending on the local circumstances.

Before you do the feasibility study it is wise to have a strategic plan in place. Strategic planning is a process of gathering widespread participation from parishioners through things like surveys and town-hall meetings so as to determine such things as the future direction of the parish and its values. This planning may also cover elements of future growth, goal setting, needs identification, program assessments, and parish vision development. If your parish has not done one recently, perhaps someone in the diocesan planning office can assist you. If you have done one but it was some time ago, then you may wish to update it, again with the help of the planning office or a planning consultant (see chap. 7 on strategic planning). As some of this may overlap with the architect's master plan, it is important to coordinate these phases.

Fund-raisers are also responsible for working with you to develop the actual financial campaign and its execution (a more detailed explanation of the capital campaign is found in chap. 13). In summary, a capital campaign normally has these major components: volunteer organization, stewardship-prayer, communication, campaign events, special group involvement, solicitation of pledges, and thanks. Volunteer recruitment is aimed at broadening the base of involvement in the campaign as well as its ownership. Campaign consultants should train, guide, and facilitate the work of the volunteers. Stewardship-prayer is the combination of the theology of stewardship together with the spirituality of prayerfully approaching this task of the campaign. Prayer is to be the foundation on which parishioners discern their role and their gift in the campaign. Communication is coordinating the web of existing and specialized tools to inform and excite the parish about the campaign. It will include the use of everything from bulletins, newsletters, and posters to web sites, videos, and color brochures. Campaign events will vary by parishes but should include pastor-parishioner dinners as the centerpiece. Other events might be in-home receptions, school rallies, and such. The goal here is to provide an opportunity for every parishioner to dialogue with the pastor about the campaign. Special group involvement is the attempt to reach out to segments of the parish that might inadvertently be left out. This could include youth, young adults, seniors, shut-ins, and any others that might be left on the fringe of a general campaign. Pledge solicitation is normally done in tiers, from the steering committee and campaign volunteers, to large donors, lead givers, and so on down through the congregation. This will need to be tailored to the individual parish so as not to offend anyone yet still build the momentum necessary for a vigorous campaign. Thanking the donors, large and small, is an important part of any campaign. This thankful expression has to be tooled to fit the personality and style of the parish in question.

Every capital fund-raising effort should include early campaign gifts from anticipated large donors. Together with your consultant you should determine parishioners who have the capacity to make substantial financial gifts. The scale of what is a substantial financial gift will vary from parish to parish. The fund-raisers together with the steering committee, regular finance committee, and parish staff should be able to compose a list of such possible donors. Then the decision should be made to call on these people individually, either the pastor alone, or the pastor with the assistance of one of the fund-raisers. The fund-raisers should coach the persons requesting donations on the methods of these contacts and should provide a script or talking notes if desired.

The general campaign often utilizes a case statement made either in letter form or in a brochure detailing the needs, plans, probable project costs, and the resulting benefits. The appeals that cannot be made in person may be solicited by a letter asking for a prayerful and committed pledge. Follow-up telephone calls may be used to secure as many responses as possible. Most campaigns ask for the pledges over a period of three to five years since a longer period of time than that usually is not as effective. The tallying of replies falls to the parish. Each contribution should be recorded, acknowledged, and confirmed by a thank-you letter. Some churches will also offer a small token gift (such as a cross, a plaque, or the like) to everyone who pledges as a thank-you and as a reminder of the ongoing nature of the campaign. Some parishes choose to compose, print, and distribute a special campaign prayer card for parishioners to use during this commitment time.

There are almost endless variations on the organization of possible elements in a capital campaign. It is not my intention to lay them all out here. That is the job of the capital campaign consultants as they design *your* campaign with you. Just be sure that you are clear as to what you expect of them and they of you. Many fund-raisers offer a menu of services for the campaign depending on your needs and desires. Some parishes with larger, experienced staffs can undertake some of these campaign tasks on their own, such as setting up dinners, producing letters, brochures, charts, graphs, etc., with only the direction and review of the campaign consultants. Other parishes may feel that the present staff cannot take on such additional responsibilities, and will want the fund-raisers to provide a more complete set of services.

One thing to remember: for something as important as this new church, I would not suggest attempting to do the capital campaign without help. Fund-raising industry statistics indicate that a church on its own without the services of a professional fund-raiser will, on average, secure only about 50 percent of its current annual giving. With the services of a professional campaign consultant, however, the results tend more in the direction of 200 percent or greater of annual giving. I have heard of one parish working with their fund-raisers to raise money for building a new church to replace an old and beloved previous church that was destroyed in a fire (fortunately not associated with the pastor!). They raised 800 percent of annual giving. Would that we all would be so successful!

Now that we have established the core job of a fund-raiser, how do you go about selecting one for your project? One key element in that selection process is the recommendation of other pastors who have used them. Nothing beats a personal referral, especially if that pastor has had some experience with fund-raising programs. This is not the only criteria because parishes and pastors differ. For example, a pastor with a smaller parish and staff might have had a fine experience with a large, by-the-book fund-raising company. But your parish may be different and in need of a more customized approach. Recommendations are important, so get as many referrals as you can and interview the pastors and lay leaders who provide the referrals. I would not recommend hiring any capital fund firm on a recommendation alone without interviewing them yourselves.

Then what should the criteria for the interview be? In many ways the categories of criteria are very similar to the ones used for interviewing the architect: the working team's track record, their processes, their style (or adaptability), the services available and fees, and the X-factor. Like the interviews for the architect, I suggest that the steering committee discuss these criteria for mutual clarity and acceptance and that interview segments are outlined and assigned to committee members in much the same way as they were for the architect interviews.

Begin with the composition of the fund-raising team. In the interview be sure to talk with the major person(s) that will be actually working on the campaign. If this is a large firm and there will be various fund-raisers responding to various tasks, be sure to meet them. Have they worked with other churches of your size and demographic before? Are they familiar with this geographic area and the manner of its population? What is their experience with steering committees? How do they propose to work with them? Ask them about the backgrounds of their support staff—survey designers, composers of case statements, letters, brochures, graphic materials.

Move on to their track record. Ask them for statistics on a variety of their campaigns—annual giving before the campaign, what their feasibility study said was possible, what they raised, what was collected, and what happened to ordinary (noncapital) giving during and after the campaign. This is necessary to discover how accurate their feasibility studies are, the ratio between amounts pledged and amounts collected, and the impact on regular giving (the "robbing Peter to pay Paul" syndrome).

Also inquire about their processes. How do they propose to do the feasibility study? How long will it take? Who and how many people will they involve? How would they gather their information? Would there be focus groups? How many? Will there be telephone interviews and how many? Will there be general parish surveys? How will these be designed and how compiled? Have they done feasibility studies for your diocese before? What is their concept of stewardship? How does prayer fit into their process? This spiritual basis will influence how they proceed.

What are the costs that are involved? Be clear about what services are wanted, and the elements that you think you can provide yourself. Be specific about who is responsible for putting out the mailings, the postage, the printing, etc. Ask for a menu of services available and the cost additions or subtractions for each. Make sure that all parties involved are clear in their expectations. This will prevent later misunderstandings.

Next is the element of style. For me this is crucial. Asking for money is an art. If done correctly it can be the matching of a need with a desire to help. If done poorly it can be a disaster that will haunt the parish for years. So listen carefully for the style of the fund-raising company. From my point of view there is nothing better than a company that has a number of formats and a wide range of experiences that they can adapt for your parish's needs.

There are some fund-raising companies that offer a singular game plan with an operational manual that lays out the steps of the campaign and the timetable for its implementation. I call these the cookie-cutter companies. They have essentially one product to sell in a we-know-best, one-size-fits-all mentality. They are often good in that they have a specific plan and procedure of execution. If, however, you think your parish does not quite fit the standard mold for whatever reasons (timing, history, personality, demographics), then you may want a slightly more adaptable approach. These singular product firms may assure you that they are flexible. They may say that they are most adaptable and able to work in a variety of styles, that they can work with you in whatever style you choose. If so, ask them for outlines of a variety of campaigns that they have directed. Compare them for real differences.

Other fund-raising companies specialize in offering a more customized approach. They are more willing to listen to your needs and wants, and they are better able to work with you and your committees to design the approach that will match your situation and your people. They can be invaluable.

This leads to the last criteria, the infamous X-factor. Do these fund-raising people seem like a match for your parish, your people, and your circumstances? Will the parishioners be comfortable with the style of this fund-raiser and how they ask for the people's hard-earned cash? Are these the right personalities to lead you through this important phase of the building process? Will they take the time and effort to get to know you, your history, and your dreams? Will they give you the personal attention necessary to make this campaign not only a financial success but also a spiritual event of renewal for and commitment to the faith community?

There is a sample fund-raiser interview form in appendix 6 (http://www.litpress.org/PDFs/new_church/appendix6.pdf). This was developed in a steering committee meeting to allow for discussion and agreement on the criteria. You would be well advised to do the same in creating your own. The same form should be used for each fund-raiser interviewed with the whole committee present for each interview if at all possible. Again, this sample form uses a ten-point scoring system (10 high and 1 low) for each category. A suggested compilation form is found in appendix 7 (http://www.litpress.org/PDFs/new_church/appendix7.pdf) for the comparison of results from different capital campaign firms interviewed.

Keep in mind that together with the selection of the architect, the choice of the right fund-raisers will be among the most important decisions to be made. The architect shapes the dream of a building; the capital campaign firm develops the means by which that dream can become a reality. So don't rush checking references, visiting with previous church committees and pastors, doing good interviews, and finding the right match for you and your people.

*Chapter 7*

# Parish Strategic Planning

For our purposes strategic planning can generally be defined as a broad-based, coordinated process of discovering the religious needs of the parishioners, as well as the planning of ministries and services designed to meet these needs in a way that clarifies and specifies the mission of the parish while also supporting its vision. So, as stated before, if your parish has not done *any* formal strategic planning before or if it has been a long time (ten years or more) since it was done, then you should implement a full-blown, professionally led ministry planning process at this time, perhaps even before proceeding with the hiring of architects and fund-raisers. This might apply in a particular way to newly created parishes that have no history of having planned together or merged parishes that have separate histories. A diocesan office of planning can be helpful with methods and trained personnel for this process or can provide references for such services.

If visioning the future, mission statement processing, and strategic planning have been done before (and fairly recently), then you should be positioned to move into a refresher and an update. As with the more complete planning process, retaining a planning consultant even for this updating is a wise move. Attempting to do this yourself can be unwise as you need the skills and the clinical distance to produce the best results. Seek the help of your past planner or the diocesan office of planning. This planning, even in the updated form, will assist you in building consensus within the parish and among parishioners for much of the work that lies ahead. For in this context strategic planning is a way to view the building project in its broadest terms, i.e., not just as a building but within the ministries and services of this faith community. That said, then let's move into the updating version as one of the first major processes after the hirings.

Back in chapter 3 you gathered numbers about future growth in the parish. You used various studies available to project what the potential attendance would look like in five, ten, and twenty years. You should have the raw numbers from this research and should reintroduce them at this junction. The point of strategic planning at this phase is to rise above just numbers and put some flesh on those numeric skeletons.

If you are building a new church, then you have probably experienced some kind of growth over the preceding years; or perhaps you have grown as the result of the merger of two or more parishes; or you are a new parish carved out of a growing area. Whatever the reason, this is the opportunity to assess present ministries, services, and programs. It will also give you a view into what the shape of needs, ministries, and programs may look like in the future. This is the chance to enlist the whole parish in a process of reassessing their overall growth, and for them together to begin to explore their future.

I would caution against skipping this step even if this has already been done. Depending on the extent and timeliness of the past strategic plan, there is much to gain from at least an updating review. If nothing else, it allows the architects and the fund-raiser to acquaint themselves with the parishioners' thoughts and desires, the flavor and variety of ministry within the parish as it has grown. This will be invaluable to them as they begin their respective tasks of developing a capital campaign and designing an architectural master plan. Only by assessing the present ministries can the fund-raiser know what is valued and cherished in the community. Only in this way can the architect assess if there is adequate space allocated to these valued programs and future ones.

There are a variety of ways to go about parish strategic planning. Most will involve some sort of a ministerial needs assessment and evaluation. If you are planning a building project beyond the church worship space, be sure to do a detailed survey of programs and services along with the facilities to accommodate them. This will require the assessment of each program's frequency of use, number of program participants, size of the rooms used, and future projections. If you are not planning a building project beyond the church space, then some of those details can be sidelined as you focus on the more liturgical ones.

The major tools for such a strategic plan usually involve gatherings like town-hall meetings, surveys and/or questionnaires, or a combination thereof. In our parish's case we had just done a major staff and ministry study (i.e., strategic plan) some three years prior to beginning the building project. This had been prompted by significant parish growth and the loss of an associate pastor, making us a one-priest parish for the foreseeable future. So with that program and ministerial staff process just behind us, we opted for a less extensive strategic-planning process. Here's how we went about it with our campaign consultant and our architects in tow.

First, we decided that we had adequate numbers from our previous analysis of growth and projections. To that we appended a profile of current parish demographics (number of households in five- and ten-year age divisions; single versus married households; the number of children of elementary age, high school, college, or beyond living at home; households over 65 years old; etc.). Watch for anything out of the ordinary that may affect or skew the future growth numbers (e.g., a higher number of families with younger children and a lower number proportionately of families with older children *might* indicate that your growth is in starter families who move on to the next house as the children grow in age or in numbers). The point here is to analyze the numbers for what they may mean, and what they can tell you about a probable future.

Next, we decided that holding a parish town-hall meeting was a good way to kick off our strategic-planning update. It would gather parishioner thoughts and feelings about the vision, purpose, and driving values of the parish as we moved into our future. At the town-hall meeting we presented the factual data of the numbers and their projected future growth. We demonstrated the increased crowding in parish Masses and services in the past five years, asking the obvious question of what we were going to do with these projected numbers when they arrived. It was important to do this clearly with numbers for each Mass time. The early Mass (our 8:00 a.m.) regulars were unaware of the extent of the serious crowding at the two later morning Masses. We laid out the givens, such as the limited number of priests and that our parish would not have a second priest (associate pastor) in the foreseeable future, the limited number of Masses a priest can celebrate on a weekend, the limited capacity of our present space, and the pros and cons of present church expansion versus a new building.

Having set the stage in this fashion, we wanted to move those attending into a larger framework of thought. We asked them to focus on the present and future of the whole parish and not just the building issues. We wanted them to concentrate on the ministries, programs, and services that make this parish what it is. These were important since we knew it wasn't our cinder-block and brick box-like structure of the church that was attracting more parishioners! We tried to elicit from them what elements and directions they cherished and wanted to preserve as we grew into our future.

After the introductions and the establishment of the scope of the meeting that was done by the pastor and members of the steering committee, the rest of the town hall was facilitated by our planning consultant with committee members functioning as scribes on newsprint sheets. The architectural working team was in attendance furiously taking notes of their own as were the fund-raisers. Here is a sampling of the topics that were given to the parishioners for input and ideas.

Purpose and mission of the parish: *What would you like to see our parish become over the next ten to twenty years? As you listened to the numbers and the demographic data, what struck or surprised you about our parish now? What are the values and beliefs that you want our parish to live by? What do you treasure most about your experience of our parish? What do we want others to experience when they come to our parish? As we grow what is your future vision for our parish and what it should be?*

Programs and services: *What social, economic, political, and technological forces will influence us most over the next ten to twenty years? Which forces will help us? Which forces will hinder us? What are the most important needs we should be addressing over the next ten to twenty years? What in these areas: Pastoral care? Liturgy? Youth education? Adult education? Sacramental services? Missions? Services for senior citizens? Services for teens? Services for children? Spiritual formation? Music in worship? Adult support groups? Social justice and community needs? Others?*

Future needs assessment and vision: *How would you describe success in each of these areas (using the same list as above)?*

Worship environment: *Given what you have just said about your vision for our parish, what would an ideal worship space for us look like? How would it sound? What would it feel like? What elements or features would it have?* (Add similar questions about social space, classroom and meeting space, office and administrative space, if these are part of the anticipated building project.)

Architectural concerns: *What would the ideal grounds/parking/landscaping space for our parish look and feel like?*

The discussion was most spirited and the meeting went well. But the attendance numbers were not what we wanted or expected. So the steering committee gathered all the information generated by that town-hall meeting, discussed and analyzed it, then created a parish survey based on it. That translated into a simple format of six questions or topic areas. This survey was distributed to each adult at all the Masses on a given weekend. Most were returned immediately. A few were mailed back the following week. Extra copies were made available for those absent to have the next weekend. Response was strong with almost eight hundred returns. They were told that the items were generated by their fellow parishioners at that town-hall meeting. The six questions were followed by five or six of the most frequent responses from the meeting, along with a write-in line for other comments. See appendix 8 for a sample of the survey we used (http://www.litpress .org/PDFs/new_church/appendix8.pdf; note: this sample is not meant to substitute for the planning process or be a shortcut; it was only one part of the whole process).

The results of the written survey were compiled and then analyzed again by the steering committee, looking this time for what we came to call value statements. Here we tried to move beyond the particulars of a program or statement to the underlying value. In fact, throughout the processes of asking the parishioners for input we tried to confine ourselves and our instruments to derive value-oriented statements. We wanted to avoid getting into detailed discussions of specific programs, ministries, and the like. And for the building we did not want the parish as a whole to focus on specifics of the new church, like particular colors, textures, architectural styles, decor, wall treatments, etc. We wanted the broader input that would anchor itself in their value statements of a more universal nature. We found that the way to discover those values often was to ask specific questions. Then the steering committee itself was responsible for distilling those particulars and extracting the core values from them. This process of eliciting broadly based values allowed us to avoid descending into petty fights over ministry (what time the parish school of religion would meet or whether Communion to shut-ins would be *before* or *after* the 10:00 a.m. Mass) or building specifics (colors, styles, decor, etc.). It did, however, give us in those values concrete particulars to incorporate.

The values echoed at this point by the number of responses in those areas queried in the survey included items like the following:

- A sense of community, friendliness, openness, welcome
- Quality homilies, good preaching, a well-done Liturgy of the Word
- Quality liturgies, music, and inclusive ministries
- The variety of parish programs and multiplicity of ministries
- Developing Catholic spirituality for today, exploring new formats
- The importance of fellowship and social opportunities
- Service to the civic community (poverty, peace, justice, community leadership)
- Care of the elderly
- Importance of a high level of parishioner involvement in services and outreach

Your items and resultant values will differ, based on your community and your survey.

Then another town-hall meeting was scheduled to report the broader parish survey results, and to solicit comments, clarifications, expansions, and, perhaps most important, to validate the conclusions flowing from the data. This in essence was a checkup on the steering committee to see if they had correctly heard and interpreted the results from the first town-hall meeting and had culled the key elements from the survey results. Again, the architects and fund-raisers attended this second town-hall meeting to observe comments and reactions, refining their feel for the parish community. They also sat in on the steering committee's values derivation discussions prior to this second town hall.

The value statements were introduced at this juncture as summations and conclusions coming from the data. Having tested the value conclusions at this second town hall, the results of the surveys, along with the value cornerstones, were published for the entire parish in a newsletter format. If you deem it appropriate, you may wish to share the tested results in a Sunday homily (see appendix 3.3, http://www.litpress.org/PDFs/new_church/appendix3.pdf) to underscore the extensive scope of the preparations for building and the importance of the programs and ministries that make up the parish. These findings were incorporated into a strategic-planning report to the diocese according to their guidelines and format.

As we leave this area, let me once more stress the importance of strategic planning, for this process lays the groundwork for the master-planning process that will be conducted by the architects. If your parish has not done strategic planning recently or at all, then for a first or a more extensive strategic-planning process, there are many resources available. Check with the diocesan office of planning for methods and a consultant to help you.

## Chapter 8

# The Architectural Master Plan

Let's move from the work of strategic planning to that of the architects. Before we tackle the topic of a master plan, let me raise the question of one more hiring in this area. There is another professional that you might want to consider selecting at this time: an acoustical engineer.

To fulfill its functions, a church must have good sound. Many wonderful churches have been ruined by poor or even outright bad acoustics. If the people can't hear the spoken word or if the sung word is flat, then all the architectural efforts are for naught. Sound is essential to a church.

The acoustical challenge of a church is the element of balance. Most buildings are designed with a singular purpose that is dominant. They are meant to be either resounding places for music such as concert halls, or they are to be places of attentiveness to the spoken word such as a true auditorium or lecture hall. The challenge of a church is that it is meant to be both. A church is a place of both word and song. The challenge for the architects is to design a space for speaking and singing within certain parameters. It must balance these two competing design requirements.

A church designed for singing is going to have a strong echo or reverberation factor. This is brought about in part by hard surfaces, sort of like the effect of singing in the shower surrounded by tile. In a church all the different hard surfaces combine to create a similar effect, from the hard surfaces of floors and walls down to the surfaces of pew backs and seats. On the other hand, a church designed for the spoken word is going to have to suppress the echo or reverberation to some extent. This can be brought about by the introduction of angular deflections, soft surfaces, sound-absorbing materials, similar to the sound dampening in a library with heavy furniture, carpet, acoustical ceiling tiles, even drapes. The point here is that everything in the space has an acoustical value and effect.

Experience had taught me that acoustical engineers are often brought in too late in the building process. Attempting to create a desired acoustic effect after a building is finalized or even already constructed can be very expensive, and at times virtually impossible. It is better to begin early in the design process with the acoustical engineering consultant working with the architect from the start.

I have even heard of situations in church construction where the acoustical engineers were not contacted until it was time to design and install a sound system with the expectation that the system would correct or balance factors that were already inherent in the design of the building. Electronics can only do so much. I didn't want to find my parish in this situation. I wanted the acoustical engineers to have a significant role in the design process from a very early phase. I wanted them on board early with our architects when items like room shape, walls, textures, surfaces, and the like began to emerge. If brought in early with the architects, acoustical engineers can be true wizards.

We hired the acoustical engineering consultants directly ourselves. They were technically an independent consultant and contractor, but they were charged with collaborating with the architects and with the parish liturgy and music director. They reported to the steering committee. Recommendations for acoustical firms were sought, references were checked, interviews were conducted by the steering committee much as in the case of the selection of architects and capital campaign consultants. See appendix 9 for a sample interview form (http://www.litpress.org/PDFs/new_church/appendix9.pdf).

Returning now to the topic of the master plan, it is here that the architects begin to focus on the larger context within which the church building is to be constructed. Just as the fund-raisers placed their specific task (raising capital) in relation to the needs and future plans, the ministries and programs, the vision and hopes of the parish, so also the architects begin their specific task (designing a church) within the broader context of the whole parish complex. This is the opportunity to study the physical needs of the buildings as they do or do not serve the present and future purposes of this faith community.

A master plan is a coordinated analysis of the present buildings and their usage, while looking down the road to the future buildings and spaces that may be needed. The temptation here may be to just add the building you presently need, i.e., the new church. What the master plan does is integrate all the present and potential buildings into an overall plan of development and anticipated usage.

Architects usually like to have client input as to the essential mission of the organization for which they are doing the master plan. They want to get to know you, your goals and visions, your ministries and services. If your architects sat in on the strategic-planning sessions with the parishioners and with the steering committee, then they should have a pretty good idea of who you are and what you do. They may need some more details about program space and usage, as well as scheduling the space. This is one of the occasions where knowing in advance what is coming may allow you to get two birds with one stone, e.g., having the architects join at least the conclusions of the strategic-planning process or its update.

Another thing to expect, if one has not been done lately, is a land survey of the property. A civil engineering survey will be necessary for the actual construction project, but here it also allows you to check property lines, building locations, drainage issues, and so forth. It gives the architects the overall lay of the land. It should also help facilitate a discussion about the adequacy of the property you now possess. As the master plan emerges with layouts for future buildings to meet future needs, the question should be addressed about having enough land.

Our situation was not that unusual. The parish had been founded in 1965 on a ten-acre site in what had been exurban farmland but then was rapidly becoming baby-boomer suburbs. The property was surrounded on two adjoining sides by public streets and on the other two adjoining sides by residential housing. A church-school-office complex, all linked to each other, had served the parish since its construction in 1967. There was also a detached rectory on the property proximate to the complex. In 1983 auxiliary additions were made to the church (more vestibule space and a cry room/daily Mass chapel) and to classrooms and nursery space. Then in 1995 a 5,000-square-foot attached office wing addition was built. There remained adequate land for the new church and for the additional parking necessary to accommodate it. When storm water retention basins were added with the new construction, however, this site would be out of space. What the master plan helped us understand was that if there were to be future buildings on this site, it would be necessary to begin to acquire some of the residential property that surrounded us. We were able to plan a best location for such additions, along with traffic access, and hence sequence the potential purchases as those houses came on the market.

With a survey completed, master planning can begin to address ideas for the best utilization of your property or site. The approach taken here is the broad scope, looking at issues like access, people flow or circulation, traffic patterns, building profiles or elevations, landscaping, etc. Be sure to take into account the noise factor or exterior acoustics (for example, you don't want a prayer garden next to a major street). Also question the architects as to what impact development and city building codes, building permit authorities, utilities, and such may have on your site as it develops. These site issues are critical and have long-lasting implications.

As these larger concepts emerge in greater clarity a variety of possible solutions will arise. These various solutions or schemes are further developed in some detail. These schemes answer some of the following questions: Will the buildings be closely or loosely clustered? Will they be attached to or detached from each other? Is access to and egress from the property singular or multiple? What impact will that have on traffic flow? Will parking be in one or in multiple lots? How will that affect the flow of people? These and many more questions should gradually coalesce into a handful of best possible schemes.

Let me share a specific example from our church building experience. One early question we had to answer was whether we wanted the new church to be attached or detached from our current complex of the existing church-school-offices. Given the general aging of the population (the baby boomers), and even though we had a nicely spread-out age demographic, we chose to attach the church to the present complex. The advantage we saw was that once a parishioner was inside they could access any other part of the complex without having to go outside again. Other parishes may choose more of a college campus style where the buildings are detached from each other and linked by sidewalks or paths. Both have their advantages and disadvantages, e.g., amount of land needed, distance from parking to a building, singular versus multiple building use.

As these schematic plans are discussed and reviewed by the steering committee, usually one will emerge as superior to the others. If you wind up with more than one, you may choose to present them some weekend after Masses with the positives and negatives of each, and ask the parishioners to help the steering committee narrow down the choices by means of a straw poll. After this straw poll the steering committee should be in a position to make a singular choice, and they should be able to articulate the reasons why this is the best choice. The people need to know that they were heard, and the whys and wherefores behind the decision.

The schematic plan that has come forward now needs more detail. As its concepts are elaborated and explained, this schematic plan will begin to move toward a preliminary design phase. As programs and ministries are reintroduced at this point, basic design concepts will start to come out. Various possible styles and the limits of existing structures will become more apparent. As the schematics of the site come into clearer focus, possible general floor plans may be introduced. Potential exterior elevations (the profile of a building) start to materialize, at least in a rough outline. You may now be ready for some perspective drawings of the entire site.

Somewhere along the way in planning for the new building, perhaps around the move from schemes to the schematic design phase, it will be important to tackle the needs of the existing buildings. What is in need of repair? What needs remodeling? What will the current church space be used for? How will it be renovated? Even if it is not possible to undertake these projects at the time of the building of the new church, at least a multiphase program can begin to develop for updating, remodeling, and renovation. The purpose of a master plan is to address all the present and future needs of the parish with a clear sequence of what to do, when to do it, and how it will fit into the overall whole.

By the end of the master-planning process, you should have the probable footprint of the new church, the site plan of the whole parish complex, a sequence of any remodeling and renovations planned to existing buildings, and the locations of any future buildings on the property and/or the sequence of adjacent purchases necessary to accommodate them. Some basic floor plans should have begun to develop along with possible elevation drawings of what the building(s) could look like (a specific design phase will follow in chap. 12). All of this needs to be communicated to the parishioners for their information and affirmation.

We chose to hold another town-hall meeting led by the architects to present the master plan to the parish. Promotion and advertising beforehand were extensive. The architects began the meeting by going back to the present parish attendance numbers and the projected growth numbers. They had developed a one-page handout sheet that listed data such as current area (in square feet) of the present church, parish hall, classrooms, offices, etc. They reported on the needs assessment regarding the use of those spaces along with the area of the total parish property, code setbacks from the street, water retention issues, etc., in order to arrive at the amount of available land for development. Then they presented what they termed the minimum area necessary for a church with a seating capacity we would need to carry us into the next fifteen to twenty years. Also presented were the minimum areas needed for present programs and for program space in the next ten to fifteen years. Finally, they presented the minimum area needed for parking (this may be a local building code issue) to accommodate vehicles in a building with this much seating capacity. This data was very helpful and eye-opening for our people.

With this background the architects moved the meeting into a synopsis of the master-planning processes, walking the parishioners through a summary of the various site utilization concepts, the possible schemes considered, and a presentation of the final scheme with rough floor plans, elevation drawings, and the overall site perspective. Then assisted by steering committee members acting as scribes with newsprint, they opened up the floor for questions, discussion, and suggestions.

This process worked very well for us. People could see how their input from the strategic-planning phase had influenced the master planning. The master plan was accepted with the proviso that this information should be communicated to the parish at large. This was done by means of a special edition of our newsletter explaining the master-planning process along with the site plan and new church highlighted and labeled. A narrative accompanied the drawing. Also included were frequently asked questions and responses (e.g., number of Masses possible, number of priests available, etc.) taken from the town-hall session itself. More feedback was solicited from parishioners. Like the town-hall meeting, responses were affirming and suggestions about details were minor in nature. A final straw poll approving the master plan was taken at all Masses one weekend. This gave us a broad ownership of the results.

With that the architects assembled the process into a report for presentation to the diocese, the building commission, and the bishop according to their guidelines and format. The next step for the architects was design development.

## Chapter 9

# The Financial Feasibility Study

The financial feasibility study is putting into practice the gospel imperative to calculate your resources beforehand lest you begin to build what you cannot finish (Luke 14:28-30).

This study is an examination by the capital campaign consultants to discover what the financial potential of the parish is. It is going to measure in some general way the two key elements of fund-raising: capacity and willingness. What capacity for giving exists in the parish by way of financial resources among the parishioners? And what is the willingness of the parishioners to contribute those resources to this capital project? In short, how much money can you expect to raise, and how should the campaign be tailored to the unique challenges that your study will reveal? This will help you plan your campaign process and your communications content.

Without such a study there are three major risks. One risk is overestimating what is possible in the parish and asking for and expecting an unrealistic amount of money. Another risk is more likely, that is, underestimating what is possible and not asking for enough money. Building a church is a once-in-a-generation event, and sacrifices are to be expected. People need to be challenged, but the challenge has to be attainable. The third risk is that the campaign you plan will not be a fit for your parish. This is the equivalent of flying through a storm without radar, or doing surgery without an X-ray. The more detailed and careful your study, the closer you will come to maximizing your results. This is not a step to pass over, rush through, or estimate by a nonprofessional unfamiliar with the field.

The study usually begins by introducing some new parish data numbers. The fund-raisers will want to know the overall number of givers and their average amounts. More important, they will want to know the number of regular parish pledgers (parishioners who annually make a financial commitment to the parish and fulfill or exceed it). They will want the ratio between the number of givers and the number of pledgers. They want to know the ratio between all donors and all registered households. They will want to factor in the timing of when the last capital fund drive was held in the parish, what it was for, and how much it raised. They may also ask about the following: Is there an annual parish operational fund drive? What does it raise in pledges? What is the ratio of pledged amounts to amounts actually collected? What have been the past three- to five-year contributions, especially increases in ordinary (noncapital) parish giving?

Next the fund-raisers will probably want to look at the parish income records for the past few years to round out their sense of the giving in this parish. What is the average and/or median weekly, monthly, and annual donation? They may want that broken down into layered amount categories with the number of parishioners in each category. How much money does the parish generate per year in excess of its ordinary needs? How long has there been a surplus and in what amounts? Has this money been saved? How much of a head start do you have on funds dedicated to or set aside for this church project already?

This is raw data that can be provided to your fund-raisers. They will generate much more data through a combination of research, interviews (in person or in focus groups), and surveys that are mailed to homes. The individual tools depend on the situation of each parish. The number of interviews conducted is usually determined by the fund-raisers based on the size of the parish, its history of past capital campaigns, and anything special about the present circumstances that might affect a capital campaign. Sometimes the interviewees are randomly selected; other times they are chosen with your help to be representative of various groups throughout the parish. The fund-raisers will let you know what they want and need. Be sure not to give them the names of only extremely supportive parishioners (sweetheart interviews). Make it a representative sample of the whole parish. Finally, before the interviews are to take place, alert the parish through the pulpit, bulletin announcements, in a mailing, and on the parish web site that a limited number of interviews authorized by the steering committee will be taking place, and that you are asking them to be honest and forthright in their responses.

The steering committee may want to ask about reviewing the survey questions (written and for use in interviews) to get a feel for what will be asked. This provides the opportunity to inquire regarding the whys and wherefores of the questions. It is also a time to help the fund-raisers refine the questions in light of any particular parish history, situations, or circumstances. But remember, the interviews are usually rather open-ended to allow the interviewees to take it wherever their comments go.

If you think the interview sample is too small, discuss this with the fund-raisers and ask for a larger number of interviews. This may increase the time and expenses. In discussing the number of interviews, this is where you have to trust the experience and competence of your fund-raising consultants. In the case of our parish of just over 1,900 households at the time, we had not had any recent capital campaigns, and there were no particular parish situations or circumstances. The fund-raisers went with thirty in-depth interviews representing specific parish constituencies.

After the interviews a survey instrument was developed for a wider audience based on the information arising out of the interviews. This was a way to sample a larger segment of the parish and at the same time find out if the interviews had been representative and broadly based. These surveys were distributed to the parish at the weekend Masses. Returned surveys totaled just over three hundred from this limited distribution. (See appendix 10, http://www.litpress.org/PDFs/new_church/appendix10.pdf, for *our* sample feasibility questionnaire; you will need to design your own in collaboration with your campaign fund-raiser.) Upon seeing these returns and collating them with the interviews, we did not feel it necessary to survey the whole parish by mail. You may want to, depending on the results.

To these parish numbers, and the results of interviews and surveys, the fund-raisers tapped into additional research data. Often this information comes from area research councils, school districts, or census bureau data about the parish area. They are gathering information within the parish boundaries on things like average and median incomes along with percentages within incremental income levels; age, education, and occupational demographics; size of household units; and so forth. They will also include the demographics of those interviewed (age, length of time in the parish, frequency of Mass attendance, etc.). All of this attempts to paint an accurate financial profile of your parish.

What you can expect from the feasibility study's report will be a lot more than a dollar amount the capital campaign consultants think you can raise. They will indeed give you that number within a range of probability. But they will include a lot more in the feasibility report that will help you design with them a successful capital campaign that is built on this feasibility study.

In our feasibility study we learned that there was a high level of trust in the pastor and the staff. They were generally held in high esteem from years of proven service. Leadership was trusted and valued. There was great affection for the parish itself as a faith community and great pride in it. These elements told us to put me, the pastor, out front in promoting the campaign drive. It also indicated that we could use staff members in the campaign, and could expect them to be well received.

Our in-depth interviews revealed that there was not only a general willingness to pledge to a new church building but, furthermore, there was a desire to help out with and volunteer for this historic project in the parish. There was broad agreement on the need for a new church. The master plan was supported as a solution and as an action plan. There was good awareness of the plans and the processes conducted to date.

Both the interviews and the written surveys were compiled with detailed anonymous summaries of comments. We specifically learned that responders wanted the building project talked about more at the announcement time setting of the Sunday Masses (where everyone present could hear) in addition to special meetings. We also discovered that the parishioners wanted any general recognition items (paperweights, coffee mugs, key rings) kept to a minimum. It became clear, however, that there was an interest in special gifts and memorials.

At the time of the interviews and the surveys the parishioners were positive and hopeful about the economy. This reinforced and supported their confidence and willingness to give to this project. At its conclusion the feasibility study told us that expectations for a capital fund drive for a new church could set a realistic goal of three times total annual parish giving (i.e., all ordinary income from envelopes, plate, Christmas, and Easter). Excluded from this amount were contributions for school support and tuition, diocesan and universal church collections, and any other pass-through revenues.

The results of the feasibility study together with all the interview and survey comments, census, and demographic data, were assembled by the fund-raisers into a report for presentation to the diocese, the building commission, and the bishop according to their guidelines and format. The next step for the fund-raisers will be the planning and execution of the actual capital campaign drive itself.

## Chapter 10

# The Liturgical Education Process

After our forays into the worlds of architectural master plans and fund-raising feasibility studies, in this chapter it should be of some comfort to return to more familiar territory. The task at hand is to present to the steering committee and the general parish an overall review of the meaning and purpose, functions and structure of our liturgical celebrations. If the people are going to be asked to participate in this task of helping to design a church worship space, then they should be given the relevant information by which they can make informed decisions and offer cogent advice. They need to have an informed understanding of the liturgies that will take place in this worship space, and the principles that underlie those liturgies.

I believe that the general principle for every aspect of the building process should be to give participants as much information as possible before asking them for their opinions. The more formed and informed those participants are, the better the chances for good, insightful input. Consultation should be preceded by education. Otherwise the input being gathered may just be the false impressions and half-truths rooted in a lack of knowledge.

It is important to take this dedicated time to address the educational component rather than to assume it. The steering committee as well as the parish are (or should be) composed of a variety of age groups. Those age groups have received varying amounts of formal education regarding the present form of our liturgy. Younger members have grown up with the revised liturgy, possibly with little or no formal explanation of its structure. Older members who transitioned from the older liturgy to the present one may or may not have had well-formed explanations for the changes. Furthermore, depending on where they were during the implementation of the liturgical reforms of the Second Vatican Council, the quality of the explanation of those reforms varied widely from parish to parish and diocese to diocese. The impetus of building a new church can create a level of motivation and participation for all age groups unlike other times in the parish. Seize this opportunity not only for the sake of building the new church but also for the sake of the general adult education and formation of the parish for years to come. This can be a time to form and unify the parishioners in a renewed and reinvigorated understanding and appreciation of the liturgy.

Who should do this? I would suggest that you seek out the services of a liturgical consultant. This might be the diocesan director of liturgy. Another resource might be a local college or seminary professor of liturgy. It might be a good idea to inquire on a more regional basis for someone with the background and temperament to communicate and relate to ordinary laypersons in this area of liturgy. The pastor may be aware of possible liturgical consultants through contacts with seminary professors and/or speakers from clergy continuing education forums. Remember, the focus is adult education of the laity, and not that of theological graduate students.

Let me say some more about the use and role of liturgical consultants. They should *not* be the person(s) designing your church. The steering committee and the parishioners are the best ones to design *their* church. In addition to being a source of education for the committee members, however, liturgical consultants can be helpful in outlining and structuring a parish-based program of liturgical education for the parishioners. They do not have to be the actual presenter for these sessions in the parish. If they are at some distance with travel expenses, or their other duties hinder their available time, you and your staff may be comfortable presenting to the parishioners the sessions that they help you develop.

Furthermore, some dioceses require that the building plans for a new church be reviewed by someone with specific liturgical expertise. Here is the opportunity to get that person on board early on in the process. This preliminary introduction to the parish through the education and interaction with committee members and parishioners will give them additional insight into the personality of the faith community as it strives to embody its values in a new building.

This process of liturgical education is important at this present juncture because you have just finished the master-planning phase with the architects, and you have moved through the feasibility study with the fund-raisers. Coming next is the architectural design development phase. For this process the steering committee should be well grounded in the principles of the liturgy. In this way they can understand the whys and wherefores of decisions and choices to be made in the new building. Hence I would suggest that you begin the education process with the steering committee members. Once they are up to speed, then they can be of help in expanding this educational process to the parish at large. They can act as hosts, as scribes for group processes, as table talk leaders, and so forth. This will not only lighten the burden on the staff but also should help other parishioners relate.

Before you begin the sessions with the steering committee, check with the diocesan liturgy office to see if they have any requirements for the liturgical education and formation of new church building committees. They may have already developed an outline or curriculum that can be incorporated with the material covered by your liturgical consultant.

There are many ways to structure and develop this liturgical material. It would be presumptive to attempt to dictate a singular format. Let me just share with you some of the things we did in our parish that seemed to work well. Our first effort with the steering committee was to do a session to review Vatican II's Constitution on the Sacred Liturgy (*Sacrosanctum Concilium*). The ideas stressed were that the liturgy was the public work of worship by and sanctification of the whole church. The document called for the liturgy to have a noble simplicity. All are to participate with knowledge and understanding. The liturgy is to have a beauty and a dignity that befits the work of our redemption that is being celebrated and carried out. As the source and summit of the church's life, the liturgy calls for the full and active participation of all.

In regard to the Eucharist, the document stresses the dual elements of Word (the Sacred Scriptures) and sacrament (the Body and Blood of the Lord) within the celebration of this sacrificial meal. Highlighted also were the liturgical cycles of Advent, Christmas, and Epiphany along with Lent, Easter, and Pentecost. Music is integral to the liturgy and should be generally participated in by all. Choirs are primarily to promote that full participation. According to this document, a pipe organ is the instrument of choice but other instruments should be accommodated. Additionally, art should not be mediocre but of a noble beauty as befits the worship of God.

Following that refresher course and our discussion of what might be some of its implications for a new church building, the next move was to contact our diocesan office of worship to speak with the director there. We learned that a set of basic educational sessions was available and required for parish church building committees. We arranged a time for the director to meet with our steering committee.

One particularly interesting session by the office of worship guided the steering committee members through a series of fill-in-the-blanks and free-association exercises based on words, images, and metaphors (from Scripture, Tradition, or personal experience). The trigger questions were: (1) Name or describe the mystery of the church; (2) Name or describe places of worship or church buildings.

A whole collage of images and phrases were named for the first, many reflecting material from Vatican II. They included the following: pilgrim people, people of God, the Body of Christ, the dwelling place of the Holy Spirit, body (head and members), city of light, Mystical Body (beyond full comprehension), a flock (of sheep with shepherd; of chicks with their mother), and the like. The second elicited items like the following: a gathering place, a tabernacle, a tent, a mountaintop, a temple, a house or home, a heavenly gate, etc. The results provided a wonderful stimulus for a discussion of ecclesiology, but also gave a measure of where the members were in their own thinking.

Another exercise was an open-ended fill-in-the-blanks sheet that began with the overarching statement: "In my humble opinion, a Catholic church building . . ." There followed a number of prompting lines: *a Catholic church building is ____; is supposed to be ____; must always be ____; should not be ____; should never be ____; can be a wonderful experience of ____; looks like ____; feels like ____; sounds like ____; says this to all who see it ____; says this to all who enter it ____*. This exercise continued to bring forth and specify a number of the values of the committee members, sparking excellent interactive discussion.

To give you a flavor of this exercise, here is an example of how one member filled in those blanks:

> In my humble opinion, a Catholic church building is *a Holy Place*; it is supposed to be *sacred yet comfortable to be in*; it must always be *people-friendly and conducive to prayer*; it should not be *a museum*; it should never be *a temple or monument*; it can be *a wonderful experience of God in the handiwork of his creatures*; it looks like *the community it houses*; it feels like *you want to be and ought to be there*; it sounds like

*a great place to listen and sing*; it says to all who see it *come in and see who we are, why we are, and what we are about*; it says to all who enter it *"And God saw that it was very good."*

Having touched base with our diocesan resources and requirements, we chose to retain the services of an outside liturgical consultant. We selected one with a doctoral degree in liturgical studies, with an extensive background in seminary and university education, and with whom I was personally familiar. The specific tasks of this liturgical consultant were to further assist the steering committee in educational endeavors for itself and the general parish, and to review the church plans at various intervals of design and development. We brought him in to spend a weekend observing the community at worship and to meet with the steering committee for another educational session.

The liturgical consultant's session with the steering committee took this tack. He began with a series of three questions. This structure was drawn from the Canadian Conference of Catholic Bishops publication, *Our Place of Worship* (1999). His first question to the group was: who are we as Roman Catholic Christians? This is answered most basically as the people of God. This parish faith community is related to the larger faith communities of the diocese, the region, the nation, and the worldwide Catholic Church. We are also related to other faith communities and to the local civic community. We are a community of evangelization and baptismal ministry. We are a community of Word and sacrament. We are a community of sacramental imagination that expresses itself in rites, traditions, and devotions.

The second question was: what do we do together? We witness, which encompasses teaching within the faith community (catechesis) while also reaching out to others outside of the faith community (evangelization). We are a people of service within the faith community itself and beyond into the larger civic community, especially service to the poor (fundamental option for the poor). We are a people of worship actively participating in the praise of the Father with his Son Jesus Christ in the Holy Spirit.

The third question was: What environs are needed to do what we do together? What kinds of places are required for catechesis and evangelization? What are the space requirements for service? And most particular to our topic here, what are our needs for ritual space, for worship, and for devotion? Given the personality of this parish or faith community, what kind of an environment is needed for a church? (Notice the connections to the strategic-planning and master-planning phases.)

All three questions need answers specific to this community. But that community also must listen to the voices of the larger communities (the diocesan and the universal churches). And they must be faithful to the physical environment of this community in the context of its present location in time and space.

Again referencing *Our Place of Worship*, our liturgical consultant suggested ten basic principles for liturgical space. (1) The active subject of liturgy is the whole assembly (priest and people) offering up the public work of the liturgy. (2) All the space of the church is sacred space, for it is the assembly that makes the place sacred. Hence there should be no barriers or barricades (e.g., handicapped access, hearing aids should be available); and there should be no large differences in space decor. (3) Simplicity facilitates a central focus. Avoid unnecessary clutter. (4) Within the whole of the church space there are major centers of prominence: the altar that nourishes us with the Body and Blood of Christ, the ambo that nourishes us with the Word of God, and the baptistry that makes us who we are as Christians. (5) Also, there are other minor focal points, for example, the presider's chair, Easter candle, reconciliation room, Stations of the Cross, statue area, etc. The tabernacle for the reservation of the Blessed Sacrament is a special focal point in a category all by itself and needs to be treated as such depending on the church layout, the existence of a chapel of reservation, and so on. (6) Liturgical furniture should be both functional and symbolic. (7) Liturgical furniture should be designed so that it occupies its own space and should not be crowded. (8) People have priority over furnishings. Don't overwhelm people with things. Avoid a monumentalism of design. (9) Care for and make specific space for other ministries, especially the musical space. Choirs and musicians are special but are still members of the assembly. (10) Catholic churches are characterized by an iconographic approach in decoration. We are a people of stories told in the works of human art. We have a rich history of color and paint, stencils and tapestries, images and statues, windows and art pieces. But remember that the church space is not built for the art, the shrines, or even the devotional spaces. Rather, it is built first and foremost for the worshiping assembly.

Regarding devotional spaces or areas, the one of primacy is that of the Blessed Sacrament. Then follow other devotions of this parish such as Mary, Joseph, a patronal saint, etc. The use and incorporation of treasured objects from the previous worship space should be encouraged as they are part of the community's identity. They have the capacity to memorialize a part of the community history and your relationship as a pilgrim people. Take care, however, that these treasured objects are refurbished in harmony with the new space. Also be on guard to avoid any tendency to create a museum by their setting or placement.

Our sessions for the steering committee with the liturgical consultant and the diocesan director of liturgy not only added to the committee's knowledge and comprehension of liturgy, but they also provided us with excellent ideas and materials so we could construct an adult education series for all parishioners. These were structured first as an adult education series to which all parishioners were invited and urged to come in order to better understand the new church and our liturgy. The sessions were held in the evenings (although a daytime offering in addition to the evening ones might have been helpful as well) once a month for four months. This provided a semester unit of adult education and was promoted heavily by pulpit, bulletin, and newsletter. After each session a summary was presented in article form in the parish newsletter that was mailed to every household.

The first general parish education session covered the goal of the sessions to better understand how form (architectural space) assists function (liturgical worship), and to identify important values and needs for the architects in the design process. With these goals clearly in mind, we moved into a discussion of ecclesiology facilitated by steering committee members (we used the fill-in-the-blank format of word-image-metaphor to describe the mystery of the church, but we could have used the questions of who are we and what do we do). Every table discussion was reported, recorded on newsprint, and discussed. Then we covered, by way of a lecture and slide pictures, a brief history of Christian worship spaces (early domestic or house church gatherings, hall churches, monastic churches, medieval cathedrals and formal basilicas, the Reformation's impact, and moving up to post–World War II modernistic forms), showing how size, history, and culture influenced the worship space of the Christian faith community through the ages.

The second general parish session began with a review of Vatican II's Constitution on the Sacred Liturgy (*Sacroscantum Concilium*) and its main principles (centrality of liturgy in the church's life, the communal nature of liturgy, the importance of understanding and participation, the place of roles, the elements of beauty and noble simplicity, etc.). On that foundation the session then outlined the structure of the first parts of the Mass or Eucharist: the gathering rites and Liturgy of the

Word. Table discussions after the structural presentations were led by steering committee members, asking what kinds of spaces are needed for these elements such as a transitional space provided by a narthex that helps people transition from the busy-ness of everyday life to a gathering place of prayer and worship, the spatial needs for proclamation of the Scriptures, acoustics, prominence, visibility, a music area for responsorials. Again, this was reported out, recorded, and discussed.

The third parish session picked up where the second had left off and went into the structure of the second part of the Mass: the Liturgy of the Eucharist and the sending or missioning rites. Again, table discussions after the presentations were led by steering committee members, exploring the spatial needs for collecting and presenting the gifts of the community; gift preparation, altar size, sanctuary accessibility, space, and flow for the communion rites, the purification of vessels; the space needs for the dismissal rites of sending or missioning, processions, the exiting of the assembly, singular or multiple exits, gathering space for fellowship, informational boards, newspapers, and magazines.

The fourth session addressed the other sacraments and rituals, again using table talk discussions led by steering committee members after informational presentations. Items covered included baptism both within and outside of Mass, the baptistry, and its use for adults at the Easter Vigil; reconciliation room furnishings and placement along with confessor locations for communal penance services; anointing of the sick space for use outside of Mass that is dignified and quiet, the location of the ambry, and places for communal anointings. A whole topic unto itself was the question of a chapel for both prayer and adoration, the placement of the tabernacle, the desire for twenty-four-hour access, etc. Many helpful architectural design ideas were developed and gathered from this discussion.

As stated earlier there are many ways to cover this component of committee and parish liturgical education and formation. Much has already been done in your parish over the past years, and continued on by your own example. It would be foolish to suggest that you are starting from zero, or that the way outlined here is the only way. The real danger in this area is to assume that all is understood, and that there is no need for a structured and focused set of learning experiences. That would be a huge pastoral mistake and a missed opportunity for the parish community's enrichment.

Whatever format you choose should be tiered. In other words, the steering committee should be formed and educated first. That experience can be used as a barometer for where the general parish might be liturgically as you design the educational components for them. Avail yourself of the steering committee and its advice in creating the content material for their fellow parishioners. Use them as helpers (table talk leaders, newsprint scribes, etc.) in the general parish liturgical education sessions.

As to the timing of these liturgical education efforts, I would recommend the sooner the better for the steering committee. Employing local talent gives a sense of community ownership and familiarity. Adding outside talent brings a sense of importance and professionalism. Consider using both. For the general parish sessions done in the format of an adult education program, I recommend offering them after the master planning and before the design development. The more liturgically educated the parish is, the more nuanced will be its contributions and participation. The parish educational sessions can be spread out or concentrated, depending on your building schedule (e.g., once a month for four or five months, or once a week for four or five weeks). And continue to remind parishioners of what they have heard so that the educational component continues throughout the months of the building process.

In whatever way you approach this task of liturgical education and formation, keep in mind that no single format will reach the number of parishioners you are interested in educating. Put the information out in various formats: day and evening adult education sessions, after Mass coffee chats, parish newsletter articles, bulletin inserts, and homilies. A series of homilies (best given during Ordinary Time so as to not disturb the liturgical cycles) can summarize, highlight, and review the ideas of liturgical education and formation treated in other more educational formats. Homilies, together with bulletin inserts and newsletter articles, are perhaps the most far-reaching formats. Just make sure to compress the information so as not to homilize too long, and be sure to give it an interior spiritual element to enhance the faith life of the congregation. A group of homily outlines that could be given during or after this liturgical education phase is found in appendix 3.4-7 (http://www.litpress.org/PDFs/new_church/appendix3.pdf).

Liturgists often quote the phrase *lex orandi lex credendi*, meaning that the law or way of praying is, or determines the law or way of believing. I would add to that: *lex orandi et lex credendi, lex aedificandi* (the law or way of praying and believing is the law or way of building).

## Chapter 11

# Church Visits and Assessments

After all these studies (liturgical, feasibility, strategic), it is time for some field trips. It is one thing to study and understand the principles of our liturgy; it is another to be able to put them into practice. This is what the steering committee now needs to do by way of concrete, practical application. I strongly recommend for this purpose a series of visits to area (even regional) churches recently constructed.

The aim here is to sharpen those liturgical principles in the context of an actual church building, constructed after Vatican II ideally, and with present materials and techniques that should be feasible to construct today. This is an opportunity to see how other faith communities of the same denomination interpreted and embodied those liturgical principles for themselves and for their needs. These field trips afford an occasion to glean some contemporary ideas for church building (historical ideas will be introduced in chap. 12 on design development). This will let the committee exercise their refreshed liturgical knowledge and prepare them for the transition into design development in the next phase.

After explaining the intent and purpose of these church visits, a list of prospective churches should be developed. Ideally, you want these churches to have been built fairly recently, say in the past five to ten years. This will assure you that the costs remain in the present-day range, and that the techniques are within the current repertoire of contractors and craftsmen. You should check with your diocesan liturgy office for a list of possible churches to visit. Check around in neighboring dioceses as well. Talk to fellow pastors, especially those who have recently led building projects. Ask your architects about recently built churches they are aware of that you might visit (it does not have to be a church they designed). You are looking for churches that come with the recommendation for having been done with an element of excellence, above-average design, and that work well as worship spaces. In our case we were willing to travel some four hours from home (by bus as a committee) to visit a recommended church. Generally speaking the churches visited should be of approximately the same seating size that you will need to build. We found some wonderful ideas (thematic direction and incorporation of treasured objects), however, in one much smaller church that we visited. So the lesson we learned was to visit quality of any size.

Once you have your list, you need a format. I would suggest developing a church assessment form. This will elicit further discussion of the elements of any church building (e.g., the landscaping of the approach to the church entrance; the vestibule or narthex; the nave or body of the church; the sanctuary—altar, ambo or pulpit, the presider area and chair; the baptistry, ambry, tabernacle; chapel of reservation; statues, images, windows, works of art). We added guideline reminders to this assessment form for each general section of the church.

Our approach was to divide the steering committee into church visitation teams of four or five members each. These teams stayed together for all the visits. The team attempted to visit their churches as a group, although at times one member might have been absent during the group visit and would have made it up alone at another time. The goal was for each team to visit every church on our list. There were ten churches on our recommendation list, and there were four teams. If the number of churches on your list is large, however, and their location or distance is problematic, then they can be allocated for visitation by a partial number of teams (but always more than one team per church). Any church with a five-star recommendation should be visited by everyone.

The basic ground rules for a visit were these. The church visit was in two parts: the tour of the building itself (sometimes calling in advance to arrange this) and attendance at the celebration of a Sunday Mass there. If necessary the parts could be separated. But any church visited had to be attended for a celebration of Mass to see how the space functioned for the people, the acoustics, the engagement in prayer, space usage, flow patterns, etc. Note taking during the tour was to follow the church assessment form outline in order to better allow for a similarity of comparison by team members and between churches. I would recommend that someone take a camera as pictures can be helpful in keeping each church and its individual elements clearly in mind. Another set of reflective questions was to be individually filled out without discussion after attending the Mass in each church.

After all church visits were completed so as not to bias any visits yet to be made by any of the teams, the entire steering committee assembled for the assessment-compilation session. Each church visited was presented by one of the visitation teams, pointing out the strengths and weaknesses they found. Then the rest of the teams joined in with their own comments. Before moving on to the next church presentation, design elements and lessons learned from this church were distilled for incorporation into our own design process when we next met with the architects. Again, the pictures by way of example were most helpful for reminding members of various particulars and for passing on ideas to the architects.

I have to say that these church visitations were extremely helpful, though I initially had my doubts, given the amount of time and travel involved. I myself as the pastor, along with the parish liturgy director and business manager (also a liturgical musician at another parish on weekends), individually joined different visitation teams and purposely kept our comments to the last so as to allow the other members to speak their minds. I found that these visits solidified the liturgical thinking of the steering committee and their ability to apply liturgical principles to an actual church space. During the visits we learned some strong positive things we wanted to duplicate. We also learned many negative things that we wanted to avoid. This part of the process certainly affirmed for me that our steering committee was fully ready for the design development stage. If it had not turned out this positively, I think I would have gone back to the liturgical education phase and repeated it with more emphasis on specific principles missed in the visitations.

There is a sample church assessment form in appendix 11 (http://www.litpress.org/PDFs/new_church/appendix11.pdf) that was printed on an 11 x 17 inch sheet and center-folded into a four-page booklet. It included the guideline reminders as well as space for notes. In appendix 12 is a sample set of reflection questions to be completed after attending a Mass in the church being visited (http://www.litpress.org/PDFs/new_church/appendix12.pdf).

*Chapter 12*

# Developing the Design of the Church

With our liturgical education refreshed and a recently applied series of church visitations completed, we now move into the area of design development. This is a twofold phase that is marked by creativity and practicality. The creative dimension is to give the building its ecclesial feel, its churchy-ness, to use a technical term. The practical elements are to assure that it is buildable at this time and in this place.

Let us address those practical elements first. The architects will pull together all the work done in the master-planning phase. This includes the present and future needs for ministry and program space as well as the community worship space. Into this they introduce their knowledge of building codes and regulations. Practical matters such as the site configuration, neighboring properties, light intrusion (e.g., from cars at night in a parking lot), storm-water retention issues, ambient noise levels, traffic flow, etc. All these issues and more have to be introduced at this point in order to consider realistic solutions.

Construction technology arises here on the practical front from both the viewpoint of affordability and sustainability. Knowing what can be built today in this locale within a reasonable budget is an essential part of the technical knowledge that the architects bring to this process. There is no point in designing a church building that you can't afford to build or a church that, once built, you can't afford to maintain for an acceptable building lifetime.

These practical aspects rarely are a focus of direct discussion. They are the backdrop or wallpaper in the minds of the architects. Normally you will become aware of them only if a specific problem arises as the designs develop.

The creative component consists of the blend of what the steering committee and the architects have heard from the parishioners as to their hopes and desires for the new church. The architects bring their creative energies, ideas, and interpretations in the light of what they have heard of the wishes and dreams of the parish. You, as the pastor of these people and as a professional ecclesiastic, bring your understanding of theology and liturgy, your knowledge of the Christian community, and your awareness of its history of worship spaces.

"Now wait a minute," I said. "I have the theology and the liturgical experience. I do know something about ecclesiology and the Christian community. But as for a history of Christian worship spaces or its architecture, I must have slept through that class. Help me out a little here."

By no means are you expected to be an expert on the history of Western church architecture. But you will be well served by at least some familiarity with this history and by an appreciation for the accomplishments of other clerical church builders in previous eras. So, here is a brief and simplified history of church architecture. A word of warning: I am neither a professional historian nor an architect. As with most things, the history of ecclesial architecture is much more complicated and nuanced than the abbreviated version presented here. To those professionals I now extend my sincere apologies for the following oversimplification. My presentation and emphases here are greatly truncated and highly selective. I am most interested in the way theology (the spiritual) was embodied—or incarnated, if you will—in the building (the physical) choices that were made. There are similar building choices that are confronting you during this design phase. Strive to embody your theology and the history for your community as previous builders embodied the theological understandings of their times.

Early Christianity had no church buildings as such. The early followers of Jesus, often a persecuted group, gathered in each other's homes. They were a small and intimate community of believers. As the community grew in numbers, the homes of more well-to-do members were chosen to host the gatherings, providing more space in which they read the letters of the apostles and broke the bread. The space in which they gathered was often the largest room in the house, an upper room that served as a small, communal dining room. Essential to the room was the common table. In more elaborate homes a covered central courtyard was occasionally used for preliminary gatherings.

This period is often referred to as the domestic church period. Critical to an understanding of this period, and to an element of our theology today, is the early Christian belief that the distinctive element of their worship was the gathering of the community, the assembly in the Spirit, the coming together of the Body of Christ—head and members—for the praise and glory of God. What they did when together was far more important than where they came together. Early Christians were not a people of temples. In fact early Christians were even accused of being atheists since they had no temples. The community and its collective actions (its communal works, that is, its liturgy) were of prime importance.

With the signing of the Edict of Milan in 313 AD, and later the conversion of the emperor Constantine, Christians moved out from under the cloud of persecution into the relative sunshine of the Roman Empire. Christianity became first a legitimate religion, and then the preferred one. Growth of the Christian community moved from steady to expansive to explosive. The numbers and the need had outstripped a domestic setting. Community buildings became a necessity. And the form of building that Christians turned to was the Roman equivalent of a town hall, the basilica (not to be confused with later classic church edifices). These basilicas were rectangular or oblong, box-like buildings with a nave and aisles, and were used for public assembly. It was a natural choice from the early Christian theology's stress on the importance of the assembly and its function. Some basilicas had served as royal banquet halls; most had been a sort of municipal building or court of justice. At one end there was often an apse, a semicircular space built out from or recessed into an end wall. Since these buildings were configured as law courts, the apse was used for the chair of a judge or magistrate. On either side of the apse were placed lecterns holding the Roman law books, hardly a long leap to an ambo or pulpit for the Christian Scriptures. In Christian use, the desk or table in front of the magistrate was moved to the center of the room to function as the *mensa*, or altar. But as crowds grew, it returned to its former place just ahead of the opening of the apse.

This period is referred to as the one of hall churches or the early basilica. First adapting existing buildings—often gifts donated by converted Roman officials—and then building their own, Christians of this period retained a sense of the importance of the assembly, adding a chair for a presider or leader of the assembly, with the focal point being the common table of the Lord's Supper, the altar. The baptistry, a round or octagonal stone pool with steps leading in and out, was located by the front door to indicate the importance of the sacrament by which one gained access to the Christian community and was welcomed to the table of the Lord.

With the decline and fall of the Roman Empire, beginning in the fifth century and its disintegration continuing into the sixth, Eastern (Constantinople) and Western (Rome) Christianity culturally drifted apart. The basilica pattern in the East continued to develop, arriving at a centralized design based on the circle, the equal-armed cross (the Greek cross), and the polygon. In the center of this structure were located the ambo, or lectern, and the altar—the Word and the sacrament. Often this space was covered by a dome, representing the dome of the heavens. Altar screens, or an iconostasis, dividing the altar area from the nave, became common, having sprung up in the early basilica phase as a way to prevent crowding around a central table or altar.

Meanwhile in the West the basilica pattern remained in its rectilinear form with nave and aisles. In both the East and the West the assembled faithful stood for the liturgy. Pews or congregational seating were not introduced, generally speaking, until the time of the Reformation in the sixteenth century. Pilgrims returning to the West from Jerusalem relayed accounts of the Church of the Holy Sepulcher, laid out on an east-west axis, the eastern point being at the presumed place of burial (the tomb) and the western point at the place of crucifixion (Mount Calvary). Pilgrims processed up a western staircase, supported by twin towers, over the locus of crucifixion and through the church to exit by the holy tomb at the east end. This east-west axis orientation, a pair of western wall towers, and the assembly facing the eastern tomb of resurrection (from which direction the Risen One would return) became strong imports from the Holy Land. Gradually, the priest-celebrant wished to also face the direction of the Rising Son with the congregation. As a result the altar was moved against the eastern wall.

As mainstream Christianity had moved into the Roman Empire, monasteries sprung up for those seeking a more rigorous following of Christ apart from the world, even if it was rapidly becoming a christianized world. Monasteries were self-contained communities. With cells or rooms for the individual monks on the perimeter, the monastic church or chapel occupied the center of the complex, often with a courtyard or central garden surrounded by a covered ambulatory. With the invasion of multiple waves of Norsemen, beginning in the ninth century for Western Europe, these self-contained (read: fortress-like) structures served their occupants and those seeking shelter there well. The monastic church interior was adapted to the needs of prayer, creating two banks of opposing pews or monastic choir stalls proximate to the altar for the chanting of the Psalms or Liturgy of the Hours. This feature translated in the cathedral church, the Western descendant of the basilica pattern, as the choir stalls there used by the clergy (cathedral canons) attached to the local bishop and his church.

So, as we leave the first Christian millennium and enter the second, what do we have? We have the importance of the following:

- The assembling community in a domed square (East) or a rectangular towered (West) building around or before an altar

- An ambo, or pulpit, for the Scriptures

- A chair, or cathedra, for the priest-presider or bishop proximate to the altar

- A baptistry—first a pool, then a font—by the entrance

All of this, if possible, was situated on an east-west axis. The space was defined by a nave with aisles and a sanctuary or altar area. The larger churches in the West had begun to introduce a third area, the chancel or monastic-like area with banks of facing choir stalls for the cathedral clergy. Where present, this chancel area often was separated from the nave by the relocation of the altar or rood screen (a large cross mounted on it or suspended from the ceiling above it). The altar had completed its migration to the wall with all, clergy and faithful alike, facing it. All the major pieces of the furnishings were in place.

The subsequent half of the next millennium's contributions saw major advances in engineering and architectural techniques, materials, and methods of construction. In the area of materials used for construction, the tenth and eleventh centuries witnessed the widespread movement away from wood and into stone. In the West the footprint or basic shape of the building found the rectangle acquiring arms or transepts, not only for the sake of the added space, but also for the sake of the symbol of a cross-shaped building. The intersection of this body and arms often gains a tower or spire of its own in addition to the western-facing front towers.

From the crowning of Charlemagne as head of the Holy Roman Empire in 800 AD, a medieval stratified society existed more than ever. As it developed, this social order was characterized by a dominant sense of hierarchy and rank, both civil and ecclesiastical. This vertical social emphasis emanated in a theology of God communicating to humankind within the confines of this building. God was made manifest here on earth in a special way within this space. Assisted by advances in engineering, the prominence of the vertical dimension of the church building increased greatly.

Prior to this period, the walls of churches (and other large structures) had to be relatively thick and massive in order to support themselves as they rose in height, and to support the roof. With the introduction of the buttress or pier (a projecting, usually square, heavy masonry structure for supporting and stabilizing a wall or building), and even more so with the flying buttress (an arch connecting a pier on the building to the ground or another pier that transfers the weight or thrust of the wall and/or roof to the ground), walls could be higher and thinner while still supporting themselves and the roof. As the buttressing allowed for the transfer of weight away from the walls themselves, larger and larger window openings could be introduced into these walls. With the windows came greater light and a more upward and airy feel to the building.

Church windows, first clear and then colored (as stained glass geometrics, then as catechetical stories from the Scriptures), began to appear in increasing numbers and complexity. Clerestory windows, high up on the wall and clear, let in light that "came down" and enlightened the space. The lancet window was long and narrow with an acute arched top. Next came the two-pointed arch window with what is called "Y-shaped" tracery (two lancet windows put together with a center mullion or vertical post), then blocks of lancet windows with multiple mullions. Window shapes and their tracery, along with their size, grew more complex and intricate as this new art developed, perhaps with the rose or circular window being the most famous today.

The increased height demanded internal supports (columns) that developed with engineering from being massive in girth to smaller and more delicate columns. Larger interior spaces required ways of spanning them. Roof and ceiling supports and treatments (called vaulting) were challenged to meet this need. From the rather simple barrel vault (a straight, continuous arch usually semicircular) to the ribbed vault (a vault supported by or decorated with arched diagonal ribs) to the complex fan vault (a concave conical vault whose ribs radiate from the point where an arch rises from its supports, like the ribs of a fan), vaulting and the intersection of various vaults became a combined art and science of creating more and more open spaces within a building.

With walls no longer needed to solely support the massive weight of the superstructure, greater complexity and detail entered the floor plans. Side aisle spaces (rectangular or apsidal) appeared with altars for cathedral clergy to celebrate their individual Masses and for devotional use by the faithful. With more space (and light) available, statues, pictures (icons), and devotional shrines increased.

In these relatively short five hundred years there was movement from what has come to be called the Romanesque (massive, bulky, and a narrow nave; dark with few windows; semicircular arches and barrel vaulting; smaller interior expanses without columns) to the Gothic (larger, taller, a wider nave; lighter with more and varied windows; pointed arches and complex vaulting; lighter columns and wider unsupported spaces; additional spaces for art and devotions).

The Renaissance, a blend of secular and religious forces, brought to the fifteenth century a rediscovery and revival of classical culture as embodied in ancient Greece and Rome. Emphasis was placed on symmetry and proportion, on geometry and regularity. The often more intuitive and irregular or complex medieval style was replaced by orderly columns and pilasters, gently sloping gables and semicircular arches. Church facades were symmetrical and orderly, organized along a vertical axis that arranged columns and arches proportionally to the entire facade. The front often was topped off with a pediment. Beginning in Florence in the fifteenth century and spreading rapidly to other Italian cities, and then eventually to the rest of Western Europe, even as far as Russia, this ideal of harmony and proportional logic presented God in the orderliness of mathematics and the forms of geometry. As it spread, each region and country altered the style to accommodate local traditions. Hence, the Renaissance style in building became geographically diversified.

The interior ideal for churches shifted from the rectangle with long naves and aisles to a more symmetrically centralized plan (recall Eastern Christianity's development of the basilica style) based on the repetition of a geometric module (such as the width of the main aisle). Saint Peter's in Rome is an example of this floor plan shift. Renaissance churches featured the return of the barrel vault as ribbed vaults disappeared. Domes appeared frequently, either external and visible or internal and as a ceiling treatment. Ceilings were often painted. Doors had square lintels with triangular pediments above. Windows were now paired and set within an arch. Stained glass declined as a dominant feature. Exterior walls were of a more finished masonry; interior walls were smooth, plastered, and finished with a white chalk-like paint. More elaborate spaces (walls and ceilings) were finished with frescoes. Statues were now set in niches or placed on plinths (bases or pedestals) versus the more integral-to-the-building style of the medieval.

The sixteenth century brought a German Augustinian priest and a period of radical change in the meaning and design of churches. With Martin Luther's stress on the Bible in the language of the people, the pulpit became the dominant feature. The altar, which had become less table-like during the entire medieval period, was replaced by the simple communion table. Altar screens, chancels, and side altars were eliminated. The baptistry migrated from the entrance of the church to the sanctuary. Often the pulpit stood above and behind the communion table. The word of God was primary. Congregational singing of hymns moved the choir (and often the organ) to the front or a close side transept. Statues, images, and stained glass windows were frequently removed.

As Protestant denominations began to build their own churches (versus remodeling Catholic churches that they took over), what emerged was a single-room style with a nave and a sanctuary containing pulpit, communion table, and baptistry with the choir nearby. The focus was on the spoken and preached word. The ability to see the minister and hear the Scriptures and sermon were paramount. The congregation was central. Images and symbols were discarded in favor of simplicity and functionalism.

As is so often the case, if your opponent or challenger zigs, then you must zag. Coming out of the Counter-Reformation Council of Trent (1545–63), which added the confessional booth to every Roman Catholic church, the Catholics emphasized precisely what the Protestants deemphasized. The Baroque period in art and architecture, beginning in the seventeenth century, was a perfect fit for this counterpoint. Baroque, with its emphasis on richness and opulence, restated the power and wealth of the Roman Church. Characterized by such things as larger-scale ceiling frescoes, gilded ornaments, detailed plaster and stucco work, etc., this was the visual counterpoint to the Protestant simplicity. Frequently promoted by the Jesuits, these broader and lighter churches with powerful central projection facades (and in Eastern Europe, various pear domes) were distinctive statements countermanding the emerging Protestant style. Rococo is fundamentally Baroque doubled down and with the introduction of sweeping curves.

There followed a series of movements within architecture (colonial, Georgian, neoclassical, Greek revival, Victorian, Gothic revival, art nouveau, art deco, etc.) that influenced church buildings, some more and some less. This brings us to the late nineteenth and twentieth centuries. The Industrial Revolution and the population migration to cities required the building of new and larger churches. New materials and engineering advancements were introduced, not unlike the advancements of almost one thousand years before this time. Iron and then steel, reinforced and then prestressed concrete, and glass are just a few of the things that began to reshape design in what has been called the modern era.

Modern architecture has been generally characterized by a recognition that with industrialization there had been a major break with an agricultural past. This was a new epoch in human history, and it deserved its own architecture. In an age characterized and increasingly defined by its machines, the efficiency of engineered design was prized. This new era was one of science and rapidly developing technology. The historical elements and architectural features of the past were either being ignored or rejected. The lines between the sacred and the profane, the religious and the secular, between interior and exterior textures, materials, and finishes, even between walls and windows (cf. curtain wall glass), between ceilings and floors were all being blurred. The primary criterion was the functional need.

In church design some want to blame the materials themselves for this reductionism to a plain simplicity. Others point to the liturgical reforms of Vatican II as the cause for turning churches into abstract sculptures. Both are in error. Modern architects were building Gothic and Renaissance churches using structural steel and reinforced concrete. And the fact is that so-called modernistic churches were being built long before the Second Vatican Council.

So, again, what was the point of all this history? You cannot, nor are you expected to, build one of these great cathedrals of the past. Rather, you are expected to lead your people in building the church for their present and their future. But that does not mean that their church cannot have some features of greatness. This cursory review is meant to acquaint you with some of the architectural and engineering features of the past that made those churches great. Nowhere is it written that you cannot select a few of those elements or features and incorporate or highlight them in your church building. Many of these features speak to people of church buildings, of that which is set aside for God's people, of the sacred. Why not use them?

With the help of your architect, you can use some elements of these past church buildings to bring a sense of design, history, and ecclesial connectedness to your building. Find the historic elements and features of the past that will work for you in a building today. Your church should not and does not have to look like a big-box Macy's store with an up-sweeping roof added; nor does it have to resemble a gabled warehouse. You have choices about the building's shape, both the footprint (rectangular, square, cruciform, octagonal, circular) and the upper structure (our church had a square-like footprint, but it had a cruciform superstructure); materials and textures (rough or smooth stone, brick, wood, or composites). You still will need a roof. Does it have to be flat? You have to have a ceiling. Must it be plain? Roof and ceiling treatments can be gabled, vaulted, arched, beamed, coffered, etc., and often for relatively little additional expense. You have to have windows. Why not consider some of the shapes and styles throughout history (we chose clear clerestory, stained glass rose, and arched clear windows with stained glass inserts from the former church). You will need columns and supports (also no supports with a large open space can be a feature); perhaps consider them becoming a feature (we used a curved arched colonnade across our exterior front, topped off with a rose window above). You need a front or facade; it is your face to the community. You will need exterior walls; maybe some buttresses or pilasters here? Towers, spires, and steeples are all elements of added height. Would they be right for your church (we used a tall steeple with a twelve-sided lantern segment)?

Armed with this brief history of church design, let's move from the general aesthetics and form of the main church to its auxiliary spaces (chapel, narthex, sacristies [both vesting and working], cry room, bridal room, usher-greeter space, etc.). It is important to process these spaces as diligently as the main body of the church before the floor plans are finalized and let for bids.

The first and most important space to consider after the sanctuary is the possibility of a prayer or eucharistic chapel. This seems to be a tradition that is returning to more and more parishes as they plan new churches or renovate older spaces. If the chapel is to be located within the basic building shell of the new church (it could also be in a portion of the old church, depending on the plans for its use, or even a free-standing structure), now is the time to think this through. Will it have a separate tabernacle or one shared with the sanctuary (perhaps in or through a common wall)? I personally prefer the use of a single tabernacle, where possible, for the unitive symbolism it conveys.

Another reason for considering a chapel is for the economies of daily Mass in a smaller space. It is much less expensive to heat and cool a chapel than a larger church. This space also can be handy for small weddings such as widow/widower couples or sacramental validations. Some other uses might include memorial services, school classroom Masses, and prayer services. For maximum flexibility I suggest using individual chairs that can be linked together. This makes the chapel space most adaptable for all kinds of devotional uses.

We chose to create a chapel space within the main shell of the building. If need be in the future, it could be removed and another 45-degree section of pews could be installed to expand seating in the main church to a full 270 degrees around the altar. Then a free-standing chapel could replace the interior one. The wall that was shared by the chapel and the church became the locus for the tabernacle, making it easily visible and prominent in the main body of the church as well as central to the chapel. Dual access to the tabernacle was accomplished by doors on two sides.

In addition, our people were asking for twenty-four-hour access to the chapel. Many still remembered the days when churches were left unlocked so people could stop by at any hour for prayer. We secured the chapel separate from the main church with access through an outer door by means of a swipe card entry system (every registered parishioner could apply for an entry card [at nominal cost], and the system was monitored by computer in case there were any problems). Security cameras inside and out, along with good exterior lighting, made this chapel attractive around the clock. In the vestibule of the chapel there was a restroom, a telephone for emergencies (long distance blocked), and a rack of prayer materials. The chapel became a highlight of the new church.

The next largest space is probably the vestibule or narthex: Is it large enough to accommodate parish socializing after the largest Mass? Is there adequate space for bulletin, newspaper, pamphlet, and booklet racks? Will there be fixed or portable kiosks for these items? Where will usher-greeters distribute bulletins? Is the space shaped so people can socialize while a clear exit path remains? Will there be a reception area for sign-ups, registrations, information, etc.? Be sure to provide electrical, telephone, and computer outlets in this area. It is a lot easier to sign people up for different events by computer. Do you want a sound system switch so overflow services can be heard out there if necessary, but can be shut off when not needed so as not to attract others during regular service times?

A vesting sacristy off the narthex for the priest-celebrant and the altar servers is the ideal location for preparing for entry processions.

Our general philosophy with these auxiliary spaces was to try to get double or multiple uses out of them. By building them slightly larger than single usage would require, we secured more space without being wasteful. Nothing is more frustrating than a room that is too small for its purpose.

Our uses for the vesting sacristy (to which we added a restroom for the celebrant) included doubling as a money-counters room on Mondays (we built a drop safe into one of the closets, concealed by a countertop and anchored into a designed concrete base). The ushers have a closet as well for their things (baskets, name badges, deposit bags, etc.). An 8-foot boat-shaped table and chairs for the counters also doubles as a small group meeting room when needed. One wall is lined with a long counter including above and below cabinets (be sure to deduct the footprint of the cabinets and vestment closets from the available floor space). One corner of the vesting sacristy has space for a couch, a matching chair, and an end table with lamp. This space was designed for a quiet meeting with people after Mass when a walk back to the office was not necessary, and for family members to rest during a church wake service. The expense was minimal and the benefits most appreciated.

A work sacristy should be located closer to the altar and sanctuary. This area should include cabinets above and below a countertop and space (and outlets) for a refrigerator for the sacramental wine. We found an apartment-sized washer and dryer a handy addition for the cleaning of purificators and corporals. Two sinks will be necessary, a work sink and a sacarium (be sure to alert the architects and the contractor of the special plumbing necessary for this sink). The water from the baptistry should also be able to be drained directly to the earth since it too has been blessed. Finally, check with your sacristan for what he or she needs and would like in the new work area.

Since our parish was doing more than one hundred baptisms a year, we felt that a cry room was appropriate. It can be accessed only from the vestibule. The rationale for this arrangement is that a baby should start off in the church with the community; if the baby gets fussy, the parents can walk him or her in the vestibule; then if the baby continues to be fussy, the parent(s) may need to sit down with him or her for a while in the cry room. This room has a direct and unobstructed view of the altar area. A restroom with changing table was added to the cry room for the convenience of the parents with small children. It has its own speaker system with volume control. The chairs are the same style as the ones in the vesting sacristy and chapel (easily used for other liturgical functions when needed) and can be linked together for an uncluttered appearance. With the addition of vertical blinds across the glass window that looks into the church and the installation of a shatterproof mirror on the restroom door, this room can also function as a space for brides and bridesmaids. By adding a couple of smaller folding tables with the chairs already there, another small-group meeting room can be created when space is at a premium.

Restrooms, though not very glamorous, are a basic necessity. Keep in mind a ratio of at least two to one for women's stalls to men's. Also, a women's restroom with the sinks in an antechamber and the stalls in another can relieve some of the congestion. And don't forget a place in both the men's and women's restrooms for a diaper-changing station of some kind.

A couple of easy-to-forget details before letting the plans go out for bid: locate any hanging points that you think you will want for banners, tapestries, wreaths (e.g., Advent and Christmas), decorative hangings, and the like. Mechanisms are available that can be built in for raising and lowering them. Consider similar kinds of hooks or hanging devices for the exterior of the building (and include the necessary electrical outlets) for any seasonal decorations. These are easily added to the plans now and are very inexpensive. Also, is a location for the ambry established yet? Will it require any special wall treatment such as a niche or lighting? A nice balancing element to an ambry is a similar installation for a Book of the Gospels. We chose to install our ambry in a lighted niche on the far right side of the reredos (the wall behind the altar) and to balance it with a similar niche for a Book of the Gospels on the left (ambo) side.

To summarize, this entire design process is to collect and analyze the many practical considerations mentioned above, along with the master-planning data and the overall aesthetics of the building inside and out. Then it is to synthesize the design goals, including appropriate historical elements and features. As various design concepts emerge, the task is to evaluate them in a dialogue of architect and steering committee. Your aim should be to work out any and all differences that may arise within the committee and to see that the expressed wishes and values of the parish are embodied in this design. Finally I suggest you present the design to the parishioners for their approval, questions and answers, input, and any suggestions. The aim is for the faith community to understand what was chosen and why.

When our design was refined to our satisfaction, and we had floor plans and elevation drawings, we held a town-hall meeting to present the design concept to the parishioners. A homily on the history of church design and architecture by way of liturgical education and background might be presented somewhere during the design development process and certainly before such a meeting. For a sample outline, see appendix 3.8 (http://www.litpress.org/PDFs/new_church/appendix3.pdf). The town hall was hosted by the steering committee who explained something of the design development process to those present. Then the architects presented the design in detail, noting the incorporation of what was gathered from the strategic- and master-planning phases. The liturgical connotations of the design were covered by the pastor.

The explanatory format that was so successful for us was a "You said X to us in the surveys, meetings, etc., by way of values, needs, and wishes. We did Y." For example: "You said that you wanted to be close to the altar. We did a fan-like design of 225 degrees with the last pew being just forty feet from the altar. You said you wanted an inviting facade beckoning others to come in and join us. We did a front with twelve windows in a combination of clear windows and stained glass. You said you wanted a space for prayer within the body of the church. We did a devotional apse with statuary off to the right side of the sanctuary." And so forth. This approach of being able to give reasons and explanations for the choices that were made and their values from which they arose was most effective. Questions were answered, suggestions were taken, and input was summarized. We concluded with an acceptance of the design with the proviso that there may be minor changes made due to construction limitations, finances, and the like.

After the meeting a four-page booklet with floor plans and elevation drawings, explanations, and frequently asked questions from the town-hall meeting was produced and mailed to all parishioners with steering committee phone numbers for questions and feedback. A deadline was set and a straw poll was conducted after all the Masses on a given weekend. The design was unanimously accepted along with very broad community ownership in that the people felt they had been more than adequately heard in the design development process.

Let me leave you with a very practical suggestion at the end of this design development phase. Once the design has been tweaked and adjusted for whatever input there may be from the parish, get a set of measured or scale drawings from the architect. Find a gymnasium or hall that is large enough to accommodate the size of the new church sanctuary. Then lay out the design of the sanctuary as drawn in full-scale life-sized dimensions. You can do this with some colored masking tapes, a string or cord, some chalk (be careful of the floor), a 100-foot tape measure, and a three-sided architect's scale ruler. A few pieces of furniture (e.g., folding tables and chairs, trash receptacles) can stand in for an altar, ambo, etc., and will give it a 3-D effect for moving people around. This may challenge your school-days geometry so see appendix 13 for some Euclidian reminders (http://www.litpress.org/PDFs/new_church/appendix13.pdf). For the sanctuary furnishings we used heavy-weight brown paper (taped together to make larger pieces as needed) cut to size and placed on the floor to represent the organ, piano, cantor's lectern, music stands, and chairs, etc. Our liturgy and music director had prepared these paper cutouts in scale for all sanctuary furnishings, either using the size of current items or estimating new ones.

Once the sanctuary floor plan is laid out (this should take only a few of you to do this part, but a warning: it is hands and knees work), assemble as many of the steering committee members as are available, along with any needed volunteers. With these people, walk through a Sunday Mass, checking for adequate space for processions (entry, exit, gospel, offertory). Do a baptism (or multiple baptisms, if that is your custom) at Mass and outside of Mass with a view to the placement of parents and godparents, families, etc. Do a wedding with full bridal party for locations and flow. Do a funeral (you can use a standard 8-foot folding table for the casket) for the same (and you might want to check a quick layout of the vestibule entrance if you have any concerns with the casket and pallbearers). Next, try Christmas with the placement of any parish crèche set and Advent wreath. Now, do all three days of the Triduum services with footwashings, processions, altar of repose, veneration of the cross, locations for the new fire, catechumenal baptisms, and so forth.

I cannot overemphasize the value of this exercise. On paper these lines are just that, lines. But laid out to scale on a floor with furnishings and people walking through ceremonies, you will find out very quickly if the aisles are wide enough (our cross aisle in front of the altar was not wide enough for communion distribution stations of both hosts and cups), if the choir area is large enough (we had underestimated the space needed for music stands and widened the steps of the tiered choir risers), if the sanctuary is accessible for the handicapped (we relocated and lengthened the ramp up to the altar platform), and so forth. The point is: at this stage to widen an aisle, enlarge a choir area, shift the ambo, or broaden the altar platform is simply a matter of lines on a piece of paper. Once construction is underway, changing those spaces and shapes gets expensive and gets expensive fast. Save yourself the headaches and costs now with an afternoon/evening steering committee floor party.

After you have done this floor exercise, try to get a feel for the scale of the furnishings that will be needed in the sanctuary. What was proportional in the previous church may not be so in this one. Nothing looks more out of place than an altar or ambo that is too large or small (usually too small) for the space in which it resides. And remember: these are symbolic community furnishings; they need to be large enough to hold their space without dwarfing either the celebrant or the worshipers. There is more on furnishings as you will see in chapter 15.

If you are unsure about the size of any other particular space (the chapel, narthex, reconciliation room, etc.), repeat this layout procedure and a walk-through exercise with that space also. The point here is to review all the interior spaces before you let to bid. That way you can avoid any additional change-order charges should you decide to move a wall or expand a space.

When the plans have been finalized and floor tested, you may want to run your design by your liturgical consultant for a final nod. With this seal of approval your schematic design plan will have to be drawn up by the architects and may have to be presented to the diocese, a building commission, or the bishop for final approval. Indicating the extent of your processing at this point, along with an explanation of "They said . . . We did," should smooth the process right along.

After final approval, the architects proceed to prepare the specifications and actual construction documents for the bidding and awarding of the contract. Meanwhile we now turn again to the fund-raisers and the capital campaign.

*Chapter 13*

# The Capital Campaign

More and more of the pieces are coming together. The master planning has led to the design development and to a schematic plan for an actual church. So also the feasibility study has had the opportunity to percolate through the minds of the fund-raisers toward the outline of a capital campaign. This process was to help you confirm that your parish had the resources available not only to begin this project but also to bring it successfully to completion. With the data gathered from their interviews and surveys, the fund-raisers have had the time to strategize toward a campaign that is uniquely suited to the personality and style of the parish. Now it is time to put that plan into action.

Every well-presented and successful capital campaign has the following parts or components. First, as we have already said, is the feasibility study summarized above and detailed in chapter 9. Then the organizing of volunteers into subcommittees with specific tasks. Although going by various names, these subcommittees should include: stewardship formation and prayer; communications, such as newsletters, bulletin inserts, banners, pulpit announcements, and even campaign videos; campaign events, most especially the opportunity for all parishioners to visit in person with the pastor and have their questions answered; special groups' involvement; solicitation and pledges; and thanking and memorializing. Let's take a look at each of these.

The recruiting of a campaign volunteer corps is one of the keys to success and can be used to flesh out the fund-raising subcommittee. This is another instance where the more people that are involved, the

greater the chances of ownership and success. The organizing and training of a volunteer corps of parishioners is one of the services among
many the fund-raisers should provide. This is a fairly easy recruiting
job in that the time commitments and the tasks themselves are clearly
defined. People want to be involved. Let them be. And remember to
involve parishioners other than the steering committee members who
will have a continuing series of other assignments to accomplish while
the capital campaign is in progress.

As with each volunteer group, the fund-raisers should meet with
them to welcome them to the campaign. This orientation meeting
should establish any structure needed for that group (namely, chair-
persons, a secretary if minutes are needed, budget and billing procedures, liaisons, etc.). This meeting should also lay out for the volunteers
the expected tasks in their specific areas, clarify the timelines, and
answer any questions that may arise. All this is often explained in a
manual provided by the fund-raisers that summarizes all this information for the different groups along with the reporting lines of accountability and clarification. Usually one meeting for each group is
sufficient. It is a good idea to select liaisons from the volunteer groups
to any established parish groups or ministry that may overlap their
work (e.g., someone from communications to the parish secretary,
someone from prayer to the staff liturgy director, someone from youth
to the staff youth minister, and so forth). This will go a long way toward
keeping everyone informed and avoiding any conflicts. The chairperson
of each volunteer group should connect with the fund-raising persons
and the steering committee. In the case of a steering committee that
had already established a communications subcommittee as indicated
in chapter 2, you might want to just meld it into this task. An alternative is to spin off a special sub-subcommittee for the task of capital
campaign communications if you think the work merits it.

Here are some of the typical tasks of each of these campaign volunteer
groups. Stewardship is the biblically based approach to our use of the
things of this world. It applies to our use of time, talents, and treasure.
Rooted in the Old Testament tradition of tithing or giving to God the
firstfruits of our labors, stewardship is the far-reaching concept that all we
have is ultimately a gift from God, whether directly from God's hands,
such as the things of the natural world, or indirectly as the products
of human talent and ingenuity, such as the things of the agricultural,
mechanical, or technological worlds. As beneficiaries and custodians of
these gifts, we are charged with their proper care and use.

Undoubtedly you have already preached on the topic of stewardship over the course of the years, especially during the annual financial drive for the ordinary operations of the parish. It is to this sense of responsibility and custodianship that you want to connect the capital drive for the new church. If you have previously laid a foundation for good stewardship, then the capital fund drive will fit right into this context.

So a significant part of your capital campaign drive for the construction of a new church will be reminding your parishioners of their duty as good stewards. They will be asked for their time and talents on the various subcommittees that are being described here related to the fund drive. And in a special way they will be asked to share their treasure, their financial support, to make this dream of a new worship space a reality.

Grounding the capital campaign in the scripturally based spirituality of stewardship and prayer is to direct this appeal onto a higher level, the level of faith and commitment. A solid campaign grows from this spiritual foundation of turning to God in gratitude for all that has been and for all that will be. It is from this grounding in spirituality and prayer that all communications flow, to which all events are dedicated, for which every special group is enlisted, and out of which all pledges and gifts will return.

A communications group for a capital campaign is responsible for the many forms of information output that are an essential part of the parish drive. Their tasks would include letters (case statement, appeals, and follow-up letters), bulletin announcements, special bulletin inserts, pulpit announcements, special newsletter editions on the campaign, web site sections on the campaign, any campaign video or photographic presentations, the campaign brochure itself, posters, banners, etc. Some of these are relatively obvious; others need more explanation. Bulletin and pulpit announcements, web site information, posters, and banners are basic and should flow from the theme of the campaign. Your fund-raisers can guide you in this area.

In my judgment the communications core of the capital campaign are the letters and newsletters devoted directly to the campaign, along with the special campaign brochure and the pastor's campaign homily. Most of these can be mailed directly to the homes of parishioners with accompanying announcements encouraging them to read, study, and pray over them.

General campaign newsletters should include a pastor's thoughts in each edition, a reminder summary of the parish's long-range plans coming out of the strategic-planning initiative, a reminder summary of the master plan along with drawings when available, the next phase in the construction process (if it has begun or will soon), and a general building timetable. Also included should be the overall fund-raising plan, its present phase and the coming one. Each newsletter should contain some stewardship education and inspiration and the when, where, and how each household will be asked to make a pledge. After commitment Sunday the newsletter should also thank those who have pledged and encourage those who are tardy to pledge now. The final newsletter can thank all donors and invite those who have not yet received their commemorative gift to pick it up.

The special campaign brochure is the place to briefly summarize again the need, the planning, and all the consultations that have gone into this project so far. Here, you are making your case for the project and exhibiting the diligence that has been exercised in planning it. The brochure should shift into presenting what has resulted from that work by way of the proposed church plan. You will want to include floor plans and elevation drawings. Show the people what they will be receiving for their generosity. This brochure is not the place to cut corners. It should be professionally printed in a four-color process. It may be a multipage brochure, depending on layout and the scale of the drawings. It should include segments from the pastor, the steering committee, along with stewardship information and expectations (charts or tables), prayers for guidance, and drawings of the new church.

Our campaign brochure (a six-page foldout, 11 x 25.5 inches) used the look and heading that had been developed for the general campaign newsletters (*Building with God*) issued during the entire building project. On the cover in one column was a letter from me, their pastor, outlining what we hoped and planned to do and setting the goal for the fund drive. Next to it was a bulleted outline of some of the features of the new building. Between the columns was a line drawing of the front of the new church. Inside on page 2 was a column on the growth of the parish from its founding to the present. Also presented was a column called "Doing It Right," which explained the need, the plan, and the stewardship challenge. Blocked in the center of the page was the campaign prayer text. Page 3 described some opportunities for special gifts, along with a chart of Incomes—Percentage Gifts per Week and Month—Total Pledge. Another column discussed the important reasons for giving. Page 4 was entirely devoted to a large-scale drawing of the floor plan of the new church; page 5 illustrated both the front elevation drawing and the entire site plan with the new parking lots. The last page had three blocks of information: one had the names of the steering committee and all other campaign committee members, another traced significant past parish milestones (founding, past pastors, dates of building projects, marker dates of household numeric growth, and the like), and the last column contained information about appreciation and donor recognition.

On the weekend before the mailing of pledge material, I strongly suggest that the pastor devote the Sunday homily to the campaign. I would suggest doing this in the format of an inspirational vision rather than a more traditional money talk. The parishioners should be led toward the spiritual benefits that a new worship space will provide. They should be able to connect with this new space over the parish generations, past and future. They should be welcomed into this new church as if they had been there all their lives. In short, they should find there the love and presence of Jesus Christ. This kind of a homily must come from the heart. It must be the pastor. It cannot be written for the pastor. It must flow out of what has been learned and experienced within the faith community. (See an example of what I did in appendix 3.9, http://www.litpress.org/PDFs/new_church/appendix3.pdf.)

There can be many campaign events, depending on the style and approach of the parish. The major campaign event is the pastor-parishioner dinners. This is an opportunity for groups of parishioners to break bread with the pastor and the steering committee that has shepherded this process along thus far. It is a time to point out the various features that will be a part of the new church design. It is also a time to personally answer their questions about the new church building, the campaign drive, and the church financing. The dinners are not the time to ask for pledges, in my judgment, although this has been done. Parishioners seem more appreciative of the time to have their concerns aired, their questions answered, and their understanding of the building itself enhanced.

These dinner events are hosted by the event group. Our parish scheduled nineteen of them to allow the groups to be small and more intimate (twenty-five to forty per dinner). Each dinner began with a half-hour hospitality time of wine and cheese. A few members of the steering committee were present at each dinner and interspersed themselves at the various tables, along with a sprinkling of staff members as their time allowed. This extended the informal discussions during the meal.

After dinner, during coffee and dessert, one of the steering committee members began by welcoming the guests again and stating the purpose for the gathering. Then I gave a brief synopsis of the features and style of the building. Next, the floor was opened up to questions, comments, and discussion. These question-and-answer sessions were usually a half hour to forty-five minutes long. Sketches, drawings, plans, and models lined the walls of the parish hall where these dinners were held.

The entire parish was invited to one of these dinners, which were scheduled over a span of about seven to eight weeks. Potential dinner dates were added, moved, or consolidated based on reservation responses. A local caterer was willing to work with us, using our own volunteers as servers (involvement and cost reduction). A singular menu for all dinners kept costs down. Besides answering questions and taking suggestions, these dinners created a very positive buzz in the parish about the new church and the campaign.

The operative concept for special group involvement is inclusion. It is important to reach out to groups outside of the parish mainstream to make them feel a part of the campaign and the building of the new church. It is important to keep shut-ins, nursing home residents, senior citizens, etc., informed, and they can become a wonderful resource to marshal in prayer for the success of the campaign. Make them a special part of the spiritual component of the fund drive. Ask them to pray for God's will and guidance, for good stewardship, and for prayerfully informed decision making. Compose some special prayers for them and print them on cards to be distributed by their extraordinary communion ministers with an explanation of their spiritual importance in the efforts of the parish.

Youth should also be involved in the campaign. Elementary school children can use this time to learn in a special way about the history of this parish community. It is a time to catechize about the important places and furnishings in a church (altar, pulpit, celebrant's chair, tabernacle, Stations of the Cross, statues, and images, etc.). They also may want to undertake a modest project to raise money for something in the new church that they can call their own (for some reason that I do not quite fathom, drinking fountains seem inordinately popular). Teens and youth should be asked to be involved. As a group they can make a valuable contribution. We asked them to be waiters and servers at the many parishioner dinners. College students who might be away at school should be kept informed about the plans and the drive. This is the new church in which many of them will be married and have their children baptized. A couple of special mailers to them are well worth the postage. The point here is to involve everyone in some way or another.

Believers have a need to give. People who believe in God, who see God as the source of all that they are and all that they have, want to acknowledge that dependence and show that gratitude in some material way. The gifts, contributions, and pledges for the construction of a new church are a unique, often once-in-a-lifetime opportunity to fulfill that need. To be a part of a generation that provides the worship space for a faith community well into the future, to build a house for the Lord and his people, is truly a privilege. Not only is it a privilege to give, but it is also a privilege to ask for donations in the name of the Lord and the family of believers.

The process of soliciting the donations and pledges for a new church is a layered one. It should begin with the members of the steering committee as the ones who know the most about the process and have been the most involved. Next would be those who are involved in the various subcommittees of the capital campaign itself. Both of these groups should be asked personally and early on in the campaign. This builds the foundation for the others.

Pledge leaders, at times referred to as ambassadors, should be recruited, trained, and enlisted to represent the parish in the task of asking for donations. They too should be an early pledging group. Then with their help you should personally approach parishioners who are being asked to be leadership donors. These are people who have some substantial means from which they are able to make a gift or a pledge. The definition of substantial means will vary from parish to parish. Typically these are the givers who are in the top 10 percent of all parish donors. They should be called on personally, informed directly that you need them in this leadership category, and given their pledge materials at the end of the call. Soliciting the actual pledge while you are there is a judgment call based on the individuals involved. Some people are comfortable making their pledge at that time; others may want more time to think it over, pray about it, and discuss it with spouse or family. Rely on the experience of your fund-raiser and the unique personality of your parish as you decide how to ask for pledges.

After the steering committee members, campaign subcommittee members, the pledge ambassadors, and the leadership donors have made their pledges, then you are ready to seek the commitment of the rest of the parishioners, usually by mail. A first appeal letter with a campaign brochure and pledge cards should be sent to the remainder of the parish. A second appeal might be mailed after about three weeks to those who have not yet responded. A third appeal can be made by a committee of ambassadors calling to ask if the materials were received and if the recipients have any questions. Scripts and answers to frequently asked questions (FAQ) are most helpful for the callers.

Promotion in order to keep the campaign in the forefront is crucial. During the weeks of our pledging process we were able to secure a full-sized bulldozer that was parked on the land (and close to the street) where the new church was to be built. As this was wintertime, the bulldozer, an ongoing reminder of the campaign, was outlined with small clear Christmas lights. Also during the first month of the pledge drive we were able to obtain the loan of a portable cement mixer (about the size of a large washing machine or so) from a local hardware store to place in the vestibule, asking parishioners to place their completed pledge cards in the barrel. Almost any promotion that gets people talking can generate enthusiasm for the drive (e.g., the thermometer to the goal amount, a ladder graphic, or a bar chart). A 3-D model of the new church done in foam board can be very helpful for people who have trouble imagining the new church from two-dimensional drawings. A more detailed model is always possible, but know that these can be rather expensive (i.e., in the thousands of dollars) if done by a professional architectural modeler. Your architect may be able to direct you to someone who can make such a model. Leave this model in a high traffic area like the vestibule or parish hall throughout the campaign and bring it out periodically thereafter.

The last component of the campaign is donor thanks and recognition. This should precipitate a formal discussion in the steering committee at the very beginning of the campaign process regarding such issues as a method of thanking donors, what special items are available for donation, the recognition of special gifts, and such. By the time that you begin the solicitation process you need to have these items decided in a clear written policy to avoid any misperceptions or misunderstandings. Be clear from the start.

Here are some helpful questions to ask yourselves and answer in your policy statement. First, will there be a general recognition gift given to all pledgers and donors to the capital campaign? Something such as a small wooden cross, a home plaque, a Bible, a special rosary, or some other memento of participation in the pledge drive? We did two things. To all those who made a pledge of any amount we gave a small wooden cross to be hung in their homes. These were simple, religious, and inexpensive. We had already heard from the people that they did not want us to do anything elaborate. Remember, this is over and above a thank-you note confirming the amount pledged, the balance, and the timing of payments.

Then for those who made a pledge of at least $5.00 per week (in 2001 dollars) for the three years of the campaign (i.e., $780.00), they were able to have their name on a laser-engraved brick that was placed in the columns of the colonnade across the front of the new church. These were actual structural bricks, saying by their presence that these are the people supporting this building. The wording was theirs up to a certain number of characters. The forms that they had to fill out were double-checked before sending to the brick company. I had to lobby intensely to keep the threshold at $5.00 per week. The steering committee saw how attractive these bricks would be and knew we could ask for a much higher amount. My argument was this: At just $5.00 per week even an elderly widow on Social Security could afford this. Such folks rarely have the opportunity to have their names on a building. The names on buildings usually go to more substantial donors. The amount stayed, and we wound up with over nine hundred engraved bricks. Even some college students got in on this challenge.

After settling the question of general recognition, the next question to address concerns what items will be available for special gifts. For us the issue was what people had a right to expect by donating to the overall construction of a church. Does or should that include an altar? A pulpit or ambo? A celebrant's chair? Tabernacle? In other words, are some or all the basic furnishings to be included in the general donations that come from everyone, or should these items be available for special donation? Different parishes will answer this question in different ways. But it is important to ask and answer the question. We chose to make the altar, the ambo, and the celebrant's chair part of the general donations. Others may decide differently. The important thing is to have the discussion, reach a consensus, settle on a policy, and make your list of items available for special gifts.

The remaining policy in this area is the issue of recognition for these special gifts. There are many formats for recognizing donors and memorializing gifts. There are wall plaques, nameplates, donor trees with brass leaves, memorial books with brass pages, and so forth. The first question you must resolve is this: will all recognitions be in a central location like the examples mentioned above, or will the recognition be affixed to the item itself? Tagging items or centralizing donors is a policy question you must decide. We chose to go with the central recognition in the format of a book built into the vestibule wall with brass pages listing all the donors of special gifts with their item, and then on the back pages, a list of all who donated anything to the building of the church. By such an approach we were able to honor all gifts, great and small, and thereby adhere more closely, we felt, to the Lord's reminder about the importance of the widow's mite (Luke 21:1-4) within the church proper. We chose to allow recognition plaques on items donated for outside areas (church sign, flag poles, statuary, prayer garden, etc.) since access to the memorial book inside would not be readily available.

Finally, regarding all furnishing (and artwork) in the sanctuary and vestibule, you want to retain the choice of design for the sake of integrity. You want all your furnishings and art items to match and be in harmony with the overall decor and plan of the building. To do otherwise is to introduce an element of chaos. If possible you may want to have the designer or artist sketches before finalizing a specific donation. (For more on furnishings, see chap. 15.)

# Chapter 14

# Construction—Getting Underway

After the architects have prepared the specifications and the construction drawings, you are ready to let for bid. Most dioceses will have a list of contractors you can select from to bid on the project. They usually have a method to qualify new contractors for the list. Most of this examination has to do with issues of insurance, bonding, past performance, and the like. Contact by letter those contractors you wish to bid on the new church construction, advising them of the project, where they can pick up the construction documents, any special qualifiers (e.g., low bid will be accepted, willingness to work with qualified subcontractors in the parish, any starting and completion time constraints, any required sequencing [e.g., new parking lot built first], and so on), and the place and deadline for the bids. The time for bidding is normally four to six weeks.

The bids are usually opened at the offices of the architect or the diocese. Present are any diocesan officials (property or construction manager, diocesan CFO, building commission chair), the pastor, the architect, and any others you may wish to invite. Contractors will send a representative. Tentative awarding of the contract is done then, pending obtaining the necessary insurance, bonding, and other qualifying documents. All bidders should be formally notified by letter of the award of the contract.

So, now you know what the new church will cost from the bid. Or do you? To arrive at the total project cost (TPC) you have to add a number of items to the contractor's bid price. Here are the other expenses that should be factored in:

- Any land costs or purchases necessary for the project
- Any utility extensions and relocations
- Testing fees (geotechnical, materials [quality control], hazardous materials)
- Building permit fees (paid to city or county)
- Architect fees
- Engineering fees, acoustical and civil, if hired separately
- Site preparation and landscaping costs, if not figured into the main contract
- A contingency fund (usually 10 percent of the contractor's bid)
- Furnishing costs, including pews, altar, tabernacle, ambo, etc. (anything not being imported from the previous church; see chap. 15)
- Refurbishing costs of relocated treasured objects from the previous church
- Sound, security, fire, phone, or computer system costs, if not in the general contract
- Organ location/relocation costs
- Any commissioned artwork
- Any diocesan assessment (cathedradicum %) on capital funds raised to pay for the building project (i.e., the increased parish income)
- Other professional fees (campaign fund-raisers, liturgical consultants, etc.)

How does this all fit with what you are seeing in the capital campaign? Are you still within your budget? Have you left yourself enough breathing room? Is your 10 percent contingency fund already spent? Things getting a little tight?

Then, welcome to the world of value engineering. This is the name given to cutting back from the original plans that were specified and bid on. It is a process of working with the architects and the awarded contractor to create alternatives to the original designs, pricing these options, evaluating them, prioritizing them, and then selecting the ones necessary to get the anticipated costs to line up with the expected revenues from the capital campaign. You might not have to do this. If your totaled costs from the expanded list above matches 90 or 95 percent (refer to past campaigns for your parish's percentage) of your pledges (not all will be fulfilled—people will move away, temporarily lose jobs, etc.—during the life span of the pledges), then you are in the clear. If not, read on.

Value engineering does not have to be the end of your parish's dream church. The key to a successful yet acceptable set of alternatives are those middle steps, evaluating and prioritizing. When the architect and the contractor come back to the steering committee, what you want to do is evaluate the proposed alternatives by a set of criteria. You need to ask (and discuss) a number of questions regarding the proffered changes: Is this structural or decorative? Can it be added easily later? Is it essential to the mission or function of our church? Did we promise this to the parish? Will it cost significantly less to do it now than it would to add it later? Do we believe parishioners will feel it is worth the money now? Is the alternative of a better quality than the originally bid item (i.e., last longer, easier to maintain, etc.)? What negative effects will occur if we do this? What positive effects will result if we do this? These questions can be placed on a matrix and answered with a yes or a no. See appendix 14 for a worksheet on evaluation and prioritization during value engineering (http://www.litpress.org/PDFs/new_church/appendix14.pdf).

Another approach to a large gap between costs and pledges is to ask the parishioners if they can extend their pledges for another year. For example, when the dreaded gap occurred for us, we asked if people could do this. A solid 75 percent could and did. It got us closer to our goal, but we still had to do the value engineering process. Sticking to the evaluate and prioritize process, along with the pledge extension, we were able to arrive within budget with our contingency fund intact and with little or no serious effects on the final building.

As you are preparing for actual construction, have your business manager begin a set of construction files. Among them should be a payment file for any professionals hired, an AOC meeting minutes file (A = architect, O = owner, C = contractor), a materials received file for items billed directly to the parish rather than to the contractor, a change order file for things added or deleted from the general contract, and files for any other vendors related to the building project (see the list of other expenses above).

Establishing (and respecting) a clear chain of communication during construction is essential to the smooth running of any building project. In construction the usual chain is owner to architect, architect to general contractor, general contractor to on-site superintendent, superintendent to foremen of the various trade crews. You should not be afraid to ask questions or raise issues informally on the site. But the place to do this formally is in the AOC meetings, respecting the chain of command.

Before construction begins it is wise to alert any neighbors. We had our business manager mail them a letter alerting them to the construction plans and estimated timetables, asking for their patience, and inviting them to call us with any problems. It was an excellent PR move. We had no neighbor problems, and in fact, they kept an eye on the site for us.

As the early stages of construction begin, there should be a formal meeting with the on-site superintendent of the general contractor. This is the time for any special requests or instructions (e.g., any restricted areas, such as school playgrounds, smoking and tobacco use by workmen, job site language, schoolchildren around the site, etc.). The job site is a hard-hat zone. Safety is paramount. Normally only the owner and perhaps the parish business manager are allowed to be on site. Clarify all these details at the outset of the project. Good relations and respect are important. This project will last between twelve and twenty-four months, depending on size. Get off on the right foot with each other. And remember whenever you visit the site to take pictures to publish in the parish bulletin and/or newsletter and for the parish archives.

As the various crafts come on site to do their work, I think it is a courtesy to meet and greet the trade foremen. It shows respect for their talent and abilities. It says that their work and their craft are appreciated and valued. With this in mind, let me close this chapter on construction with a story.

There is a statue in the chapel of the cathedral at Rouen in France. The chapel, *Chapelle du Bâtiment*, is dedicated to the building trades and craftsmen who rebuilt the church after a catastrophic fire around 1200 AD. Depicted by the statue are the Virgin Mary holding the Christ Child in her arms. Jesus is clutching a carpenter's square in his hand. Kneeling before them are two medieval workmen holding up a model of the rebuilt cathedral as an offering to Jesus and Mary. Below the workmen, at their feet, are the tools of many crafts and trades that restored the church. This statue depicts a very catholic theology of work, that the ordinary, daily work of these men was a sacred offering to God. Workers complete and compliment the divine work of creation. Workers share in the divine energy of the Creator. Their work is holy because it flows from them in the image and likeness of God. Work that is for God and for God's people is a sacred offering in God's sight. The work and the workers, whether today or in the thirteenth century, possess a dignity and majesty that makes their construction ("the work of human hands") and their efforts holy.

This understanding of work and the workers should inform the celebration of the groundbreaking. The bishop could be invited to attend along with the pastor, steering committee members, parishioners (including perhaps the youngest baptized infant and the oldest adult parishioner able to attend), the architects, and the contractor. Prayers should focus on asking God's blessings on the project itself, the safety of the workers, the up-building of the community by this structure, and that God's providence may cause it all to reflect God's glory. (For other celebrations during construction, see chap. 18).

In addition to the usual ceremonies of groundbreaking we took the opportunity to lay out the basic outline of the new building with chalk lines (see if the local high school will lend you their football/soccer field chalker). This required a little field work, the measured drawings of the building's footprint, a 100-foot measuring tape, and some general field geometry. This might become a scout or youth group project. Our layout was on an existing parking lot and an athletic field. It was well worth the time and effort as it gave the parishioners a real-life sense of the size and location of the new church building.

## Chapter 15

# Interior Decor and Furnishings

As the construction of the building gets underway, the architect's attention will turn to the finishing of the interior spaces. This includes materials, textures, colors, and so forth. This part of the process is usually led by their commercial interior design person. Having checked and rechecked the interior spaces as you did in chapter 12, now is the time to activate your furnishing subcommittee. Together with the architect's interior design person, they are ready to address these choices for the entire building.

There are a myriad of choices that will have to be made: tile, carpet, fabric, wallpaper, wood, sheetrock, stone, slate, etc. It is at this juncture that you want to call in the acoustical engineer so that the parameters of the surface choices can be determined. The committee members and the interior design person should be involved in this process so that all will know the reasons for the choices that are made. Take your time so that you achieve the coordinated look of beauty and noble taste that is your goal. Be sure to give special attention to the visual space and/ or the reredos, as it will become the focal backdrop to the altar. We chose a natural rock surface on a concave wall with blind mortar joints, a large crucifix mounted atop, and flanked on each side by slate-tiled walls (all materials native to our state).

While the interior design person is working on a palette of colors and texture selections, you want to turn with your furnishings subcommittee to the largest furnishing of all, the pews. There are a number of regional and national pew companies. Ask the architect, the diocesan building commission, and other pastors who have built recently for recommendations. Interview each company before making a selection. Ask about their on-time delivery record, installation time needed, design services provided, deposits, payment schedules, and warranty details. The sooner you can settle on a company and a product, the sooner you may be able to lock in a price with a deposit. Moving on this early saved us from two 10 percent price increases.

As for the pews themselves, the first choice is material: particleboard, flakeboard, or MDF (medium-density fiberboard) are the most common. These differ in the wood product that is chosen for combination with resins and formed into sheets under temperature and pressure. These are all veneered and can be stained to match whatever color is chosen by the architects (have the pew company and architects communicate directly for color matches). The cost and distortion of natural wood makes it an unsuitable and impractical medium for pews. We chose the MDF material. Kneeler frames can be constructed of wood or metal. We chose metal for durability. If the kneelers are to be padded, there will be material and color choices here as well.

Pews can be open-ended (the least expensive) or have a wooden endcap in a variety of styles that can be decorated with engravings or carvings, perhaps a symbol of the parish (e.g., for a St. Patrick's parish, a laser engraved Celtic cross design perhaps). Pews can also be upholstered or not; and for the upholstered pews, it can be seat only, seat and back, or seat, back, and back of back. Along with the choices for floors and walls, the pews are a major acoustical element. Upholstered pews give a more even and consistent sound when the church is partially occupied. Once more, consult your acoustical engineer. For padded or cushioned pews, the foam is graded by its density and priced accordingly. Look for density and load compression (ILD) numbers for comparison purposes. There are a range of fabrics for upholstering the pews that are classified by their durability and complexity of design. Include the interior design person when making these color choices. Also be sure to order extra fabric (e.g., two to four times the length of your longest pew) for accident repairs.

While you are pricing pews, be sure to price matching (in construction, wood trim, and fabric) chairs with kneelers (if there is to be a chapel) and without (cry room, vesting sacristy, and possibly the choir area; we found that with the choir on poured concrete step risers, individual chairs worked better than pews for their arrangement and flexibility). Seat and back padding and fabrics usually match the pews. Don't forget hymnal book racks on the pews and chairs for the chapel and cry room.

The placement of the pews (and how they are counted for unofficial seating capacity) raises two more questions: width and pitch. Width is the amount of space, on average, that is allotted for seating a person. A standard seating width is often figured at 16 inches. You may want to use something more along the line of 18 to 20 inches for calculating the actual (unofficial) seating capacity of the pews in your new church. Keep in mind that a church occupied at 85 percent is perceived by the average person as full.

Pitch is the distance between the rows of pews measured from the same two points on the two pews (note: this is not the leg room amount). This dimension will dictate knee room. Measure the pews you now have. Do they allow adequate knee room while seated (don't forget hymnal racks)? Is there adequate leg and foot room while kneeling (distance to the uplifted kneeler behind you)? And is there enough knee room while seated for another person to pass by? Pitch can vary from the 31 or 32 inches (for economy seats in airplanes) upward. Pitch for church pews should be 36 to 38 inches for comfortable access and egress. Remember, the larger the pitch dimension the fewer the number of rows of pews, and your seating capacity. Work this out closely with your architect and the pew company for what you require, balancing comfort with need.

There are pew companies that have furniture-design artists on their staffs whose services are available to pew-purchasing customers to assist in developing a coordinated set of church furnishings at little or no additional charge. This design service can be a great help and a cost saver. They will work with you to design the furnishings. The pew company can make the pieces themselves or give you the sketches for crafting elsewhere. We found that this invaluable service greatly assisted us in coordinating styles for the different pieces and was more than cost competitive. If your needs and personalities match, consider adding this design artist to the furnishings subcommittee along with the architect's interior design director.

Before beginning on the other furnishings after the pews, it is wise to work up a set of guidelines with and for the subcommittee. Some of these will apply to the interior choices as well. Here are some questions you might use to develop your own guidelines.

Materials come first: Is it of good quality? Is it durable? Is it functional? Is it fitting for a church? Is the material authentic (versus faux, e.g., plastic columns)? Does this material relate well to the other materials in the church? Next come the artistic questions: Does this piece have artistic merit? Is it good art, well crafted, honest? Is the scale correct for this size of space and for the humans who will use it? Is it beautiful? Will this item draw people closer to the sacraments that are being celebrated? Closer to Christ? Closer to God? Will it appeal to our people? Will this appeal facilitate the celebration of the liturgy or distract from it? Is it somehow distinctive (i.e., different from the everyday)?

There is a list of church furnishings that can be found in appendix 15 (http://www.litpress.org/PDFs/new_church/appendix15.pdf). Use this as a reminder of the items that you will need. (Vessels are not included.) Furnishing pieces being transferred from the old church should be brought to the attention of the interior designer and the design artist. They can be very helpful in suggesting any refurbishing necessary and be very creative about the use of treasured objects from the old church.

An example: We had some wood-carved Stations of the Cross that hung on the wall of the old church. They were polychromatic figures and artistic, but they were much too small for the scale of the new church. The pew company design artist suggested we mount them on slate columns (thematically tying them into the secondary wall behind the altar and its slate). The columns were placed along two side walls of the new church, protruding just a couple of inches and each making a distinctive pilaster. This solution gave the old but refurbished Stations a new weight and scale on these slate columns that made them a treasured transfer to the new church, and at a significant savings from the cost of new Stations.

With your main pieces (altar, ambo, celebrant's chair, tabernacle [could be a different style to make it more distinctive], candle stands, credence table, gift table) a theme is most helpful. The theme that emerged for us was that of the Roman arch. We had been somewhat inspired by the parish's namesake (St. Mark's in Venice, Italy) in the creation of our arched colonnade across the front of the building. The design artist suggested we carry that arch inside to some of the furnishings. Arches and blind arches (arches outlined on a vertical surface) were applied to these main pieces of furniture with great success, not only tying the pieces together but also linking them to the architecture of the building itself.

Once the furnishings have been designed and the subcommittee has signed off on them, you may want to ask the design artist if you can have copies of the sketches (not the measured fabrication drawings). Put these sketches together into a brochure or booklet, thereby creating a contributor's list of items available for special donation, dedication, and memorialization. These furnishings are always more attractive to the donors when they can be seen and envisioned as parts of a whole set. You might want to work with your capital campaign person for setting amounts on each piece.

As we close out this chapter on interior furnishings, it might be wise for you to review chapter 12 for its ideas about the tabernacle, ambry, vestibule furniture, sacristy furnishings and casework (cabinets), etc. With all church furniture you are trying to blend artistic function (its symbolism and scale for community celebrations) with practical function (its utility for people).

## Chapter 16

# Original Artwork

The church has a long and mostly admirable history of being a patron of the arts. In their work for the church, artists share in a special way the creative task of the Lord. Their efforts and energies are capable of producing beautiful and noble works that serve the Christian people in their worship of God.

> For that reason the church has always been a friend of the fine arts, has ever sought their noble ministry and has trained artists. Its chief purpose has been to ensure that all things set apart for use in divine worship should be worthy, becoming, and beautiful, signs and symbols of things supernatural. (The Constitution on the Sacred Liturgy, *Sacrosanctum Concilium*, 122)

With this in mind, it is my opinion that you should strive for some original works of art in your new church. There are plenty of commercially produced pieces of church art (statues, images, furnishings, etc.). Here is an opportunity to create something unique and special to this parish. From where will the next generation of religious art (and artists) come? Should it be cathedrals only? Does not the local church have a role to play in this endeavor? I think it does. For too long we have relied almost exclusively on catalog religious art at the parish level.

Though you may be able to afford only one or two pieces of original artwork, it is well worth the expense in terms of the ownership and pride it can generate within the faith community. If the budget is

stretched thin, this may be a place to seek special or memorial donations to make this artwork possible. The sponsorship can be by an
individual or by groups in the parish already existing or newly consti-
tuted for this purpose (our Mary statue was the gift of one person; we
bought the Joseph statue with many small donations from over two
hundred parishioners). You may be pleasantly surprised by the interest
in some original artwork.

Once the steering committee has discussed the possibility, then it is
time to activate the artwork subcommittee. Their first task should be to
identify items that could be considered for original artwork. Here are
some of the obvious things to begin to examine as possible candidates:
the tabernacle, the main crucifix, statues (Mary, Joseph, the parish's
patron), Stations of the Cross (bas-relief, paintings, carvings), stained
glass windows, etched glass works, exterior statues, etc.

Once you have identified some possible pieces, give some thought
to the medium or material. At least initially, in what type of materials
do you envision the pieces being created? Stone (natural or artificial),
bronze (hot or cold cast), other metals, wood, resins? To some extent
the material may determine to which artists you look. Some artists
work in only a certain medium; others are comfortable in a variety of
materials. If you decide on a particular medium—stone, for example—
then there is no point in interviewing artists that work only in bronze.
I caution you against determining the material too early in this process,
unless you are bound to a particular medium by other treasured objects
that are being transferred from the former worship space. If you have
multiple pieces to be created, you may be working with more than one
artist. Just make sure their styles and media are complimentary if they
are to occupy proximate spaces.

Selecting an artist is in many ways like selecting the architect.
You are looking for a marriage of talent and understanding—talent
to produce a work of art and understanding of the community with
its needs and desires. Like architects, you will want to ask around for
recommendations and references. Talk to other pastors who have built
or commissioned pieces recently. The diocesan building commission
or ones from neighboring dioceses might have recommendations. Also
investigate your and neighboring offices of worship. The architects may
have a listing of artists they have worked with in the past. Explore any
local university or art schools for ideas. Ask the parishioners, but be
sure they understand that you are looking for professional artists capable of commercial-grade pieces.

Once you have a list, send out a letter stating what you are interested in (number and types of pieces, the medium if already selected, general size, and your timetable). Ask the artists to submit a portfolio of their work. Review these carefully, taking particular note of styles, textures, and media. Check all references from past work as to how they related with building committee members, their responsiveness to all communications, their acceptance of input and requests for changes, their willingness to preview work to the parish, timeliness, and the possibility of extra charges above the quoted price (shipping, delivery, installation, trips to the location, model costs, guarantees of materials and workmanship).

If you have a number of artists you are considering who happen to be at a considerable distance from you, you may want to use telephone interviews as an intermediate step after seeing their portfolios and before the face-to-face interviews. When you have your list winnowed down to the candidates you are most interested in, you should interview them in person. Like other selection interviews, have a script prepared from the subcommittee's discussion of the criteria. Try to keep the artists' interviews as close together as possible for the freshness of impressions.

For the interview ask them to bring pictures or models and explain a couple of past works they have created, including a description of why they did what they did. Ask them to speak to the various media (stone, metal, wood, other) and which they prefer, or the characteristics of each one. Ask them about possible textures for your various pieces. Which media and texture would they recommend for your intended pieces and why? Ask for an approximate price quote for each intended piece.

As the interview is taking place, ask yourself if you (and the committee) can work with this person. Are they able to give you what you want versus what they want? Are they open to feedback and input on a work in progress? If not, can they explain their position and reasons clearly and courteously? Is their style within the range of this community of people? Does this artist have a variety and depth of styles in a variety of media?

Does their work stir emotions? Does each look unique versus mass-produced? Do their works allow for a range of interpretations? Will their works or style enhance prayer or distract from it? Will they work with you all along the way, from sketches to miniature models to pictures before actual castings? Do they see the artwork as a blend of them and the community? Are they willing and able (time, distance, workload) to get to know this community for which they are creating the artwork?

Your artwork subcommittee should discuss these criteria, adding and subtracting what is particular to your community, and then create an artist interview form. The interviews may differ in depth, depending on the work of art, the knowledge of the designer, and if the interviewee is both the designer and the fabricator. See appendices 16 (http://www.litpress.org/PDFs/new_church/appendix16.pdf) and 17 (http://www.litpress.org/PDFs/new_church/appendix17.pdf) for sample interview and compilation forms.

Let me give you a few examples from our experience that may help guide you in this process of collaborating on original artwork. Believe me, I had no background or previous experience in this area at all. All I knew was that Vatican II had encouraged us to involve ourselves in creating new works of art. Our initial focus was to list what might be possible original artwork in our new church. Most were in the area of statues. Our steering committee's artwork wish list follows in order of priority, as we were not sure how the financial response would be: the tabernacle, the main crucifix, Mary statue, Joseph statue, stained glass rose window(s), patronal statue (outdoors), prayer garden bas-relief plaques, a reliquary. Certainly a long list, but we felt that some items could be added at a later date as funds became available.

The first artist chosen was for the tabernacle. In our case he happened to be the design artist from the pew and furnishings company, a most creative individual. We had no firm ideas about a tabernacle. As it was to be located between the chapel and the main sanctuary (and accessible from both sides), he suggested a composition of wood and glass on a wooden pedestal stand. The tabernacle would be placed into a tall Romanesque arch in the wall, and surrounded by a leptat glass panel that would fill the arch. On the chapel side a sanctuary lamp would hang, visible from the sanctuary through the glass arch. The tabernacle, a square column with a hipped roof and dual doors, was fabricated of red oak and then covered in leptat glass. Leptat is a deeply etched glass, using a leptat acid process (versus an abrasive process for frosting glass). It produces a more crystal-like product with varied surfaces. These crystal-like surfaces catch and reflect light rays from more angles, like a precious jewel. Both the tabernacle and glass panel were finished in a pattern of grapes and wheat that was most powerful.

Since this was being designed by the person doing the interior furnishings, we were highly confident that it would be complementary to the other furnishings from the same hand. We simply displayed the sketches of the tabernacle for the community's information as other furnishing sketches became available.

Our second artist was selected through the interview process. In this case we were looking for someone able to create statuary. We began the statuary pieces with the main crucifix. Behind the altar was a natural rock concave wall (reredos) designed by the architects. By inclining the top upward toward the center, the illusion of a rocky hill was created. The plan that emerged was to place a large wooden cross atop the wall. The corpus needed to be slightly larger than life due to scale and elevation (e.g., the eyes of the corpus would be some twenty-four feet above the floor). This crucifix would become a dominant visual feature above and behind the altar.

As to the figure of the corpus, we chose to seek the input of the community. Following an educational homily about statuary (see appendix 3.10, http://www.litpress.org/PDFs/new_church/appendix3.pdf), committee members casually asked parishioners after Mass how they imagined Jesus on the cross. The overall preference was for Jesus still alive, looking up to the Father from the cross. The desired expression was one that would accommodate a variety of meanings as in the traditional Seven Words from the cross. This turned out to be a wonderful approach: allow people to identify with Jesus in what they bring to the cross in prayer—fear, loneliness, anguish, loss, gratitude, hope. We chose cold-cast bronze to alleviate the weight suspension problem. The texture was smooth, the color was burnished antique gold, the wood was red oak hollowed out to receive the corpus. A miniature corpus was created by the artist and enthusiastically received by the congregation. The cost was absorbed in the furnishings budget as it was felt that it belonged to the basic furnishings of a new church.

The Mary and Joseph statues were to be created by the same artist. He had visited the parish community (and the committee) a couple of times to get a feel for the people, their Sunday worship together, and to hear their suggestions. With that casual input and observation and by working with the committee, he came up with the concept of a Mary statue seated in prayer, inviting the viewer to join with her. She was placed, life-sized, on a simple two-person wooden bench like what might have been in a carpenter's home. People could sit next to her or kneel at her feet on a platform. Children could crawl up in her lap. It was a most approachable Mary, inviting closeness, touch, and interaction. As this was a somewhat nontraditional statue (not the typical pedestal-posed statue), the committee recommended a small model test. The artist created one, and the committee displayed it for a couple of weekends and invited reactions. With few exceptions, and backed by the statue homily, this Mary won a large majority of hearts. Mary was cast in cold bronze, matching the corpus in texture and color. Finding a sponsor was little trouble with this attractive figure. Note here the difference in processes: after general education and information on statuary, the people were consulted on the corpus for a desired style and expression, whereas a preconceived Mary statue was presented for reaction and acceptance. Both processes can work well.

The Joseph statue took another creation pathway. While touring in Budapest, Hungary, I happened to see a statue of Joseph in the *Belvárosi Plébániatemplom* (the inner-city parish church) and brought home a picture of it. Joseph was seated in a high-backed chair with a five-year-old Jesus at his knee, holding a carpenter's square as if to say, "How do I use this?" It was the first time I had seen a Joseph statue teaching Jesus. I thought it was a powerful image for a father and child. I presented this to the committee and they agreed. We asked the artist to work within this sort of concept.

Beginning with a tool-strewn workbench, Joseph is on one knee with his arm resting on the bench. Jesus is across a corner of the bench from Joseph holding up a block plane and asking for helpful instruction. The observer creates the third point of an interactive triangle made up of Jesus, Joseph, and that person. Then the question arises: Are you the father (parent) with your child like Joseph and Jesus? Or are you the child with your father (parent)? Is this you as mentor? Are you the one being mentored? This statue invites meditation and reflection on many levels. An upholstered bench was provided facing the statue, yet some people choose to kneel on the platform. Children liked the size and approachability of a young Jesus.

Again, a small model of the Joseph statue was put out for testing and found acceptable. Joseph too was cast in cold bronze, matching the corpus in texture and color. The workbench was a casting in cold bronze of an old, well-worn workbench top with tools molded into the surface. In this case there was not a single donor as with the Mary statue, but a spontaneous outpouring of small donations from many (some 240!) parishioners made this statue a reality.

Outdoors we wanted a statue of our patron saint, St. Mark the Evangelist, to be created by the same artist that did the above three figures. This one was to be about life-size in hot-cast bronze to withstand the weather. It was to be placed in a centered niche in a protruding apse wall. This was to be a focal point for those approaching the church from the side parking lot. Since the statue would face north, the artist suggested we give Mark windblown hair and beard (remember Moses on the mountain in the movie *The Ten Commandments* in the 1950s?). Holding the scroll (not a book, as we wanted all our art pieces to be historically probable) of his gospel with the initial words in Greek, Mark boldly proclaims this building to be one of "Jesus Christ, the Son of God." Processes here were minimal other than to display a small model for the information and input of the parish. There was very little in this case as St. Mark is rarely portrayed except in symbolic form as the winged lion. A single sponsor came forward to donate for this outdoor statue.

The third artist was chosen for the bas-relief sculptures in the prayer garden. More on this is covered in chapter 17 on landscaping. The interviewing, theme setting, model reviews, etc., for this artist followed the processes outlined above for the statues.

We used the design artist from the pew and furnishings company again for the stained glass windows (do you get a sense of how important the selection of the pew company and its talent pool was to our endeavor?). We asked him if he would work with our subcommittee to produce the designs for four stained glass windows for an additional fee. These were to be circular rose windows, approximately 8 feet in diameter, below the gables of the four end walls that make up the cruciform superstructure of the church. We had no preconceived theme or images for these windows. Their fabrication was to be done separately from the pew company. In fact, we found a local stained glass company just a mile from the church to make them, and they did a fantastic job.

As the four walls each faced a cardinal point on the compass, the artist suggested a seasonal theme that would incorporate aspects of the Eucharist. Working together with the committee, the artist designed seasonal hues for each window (north—cool, pale, snow-like; south—vibrant greens of summer; east—pastel blues of a spring sky; west—harvest golds). The themes that developed for the windows were the multiplication of loaves and fishes in the north, the hands of the sower sowing seed in the south, the great catch in the morning fishermen's boat in the east, and the great harvest of stalks of wheat and bunches of grapes in the west. Bordering each window to tie all four together were vines and branches. Sponsors were found for each window with little delay. All were created and installed by dedication, although they could have been executed as funds became available.

Our last art piece was a reliquary. The parish had acquired earlier a first-class relic of St. Mark the Evangelist, and after discussion in the artwork subcommittee, the choice was made to display it rather than encase it beneath the altar table. The floor plans called for a devotional apse to the right of the sanctuary and church nave. This was to be the location of the Mary and Joseph statues, and it had a chair rail lined with small votive candles. A wide center pilaster provided the location for a wall-mounted, wood and stained glass relic house with a central clear glass panel through which the relic itself was displayed. It was perimeter-lighted from within, locked for security (yet removable if necessary), and with a vigil light of its own. Thus this apse, technically apart from the sanctuary yet most accessible before and after Mass, with its statues and relic became a popular candle-lit devotional area for prayer.

All of our artists were filled with excellent ideas, open to hearing our suggestions, and willing to work with our artwork subcommittee, which I attribute to good interviewing processes. It was in that interplay of talents and ideas that a number of newly treasured works of art arose for our new church, and can for yours.

## Chapter 17

# Landscaping and a Prayer Garden

The time has come to look outdoors at the landscaping and the external spaces around the church. Landscaping can be done by the general contractor, by a separate landscape contractor apart from the general bid, or by a combination of the two (the general doing what is required by the building codes, and the landscaper doing the more creative dimensions). When the landscaping is included in the general bid and done solely by the general contractor, it is typically the more basic type unless your architect has called for a specific landscaping plan already. Contractor landscaping usually includes the cleanup of the site after construction, laying sod or sowing grass seed as set by the specifications, and planting trees, bushes, and shrubs. In some cases the number of trees and plantings will be dictated by the local building codes. The architect will be aware of these requirements for your area.

If there are local landscape contractors in your area and you would like to make this element of the new church a bit more creative, you may want to consider bidding out some of this work separately from the general contract. It could be more cost-effective and allow for greater detail. In this case, have the general contractor do the cleanup and any significant ground contouring, and then turn it over to the landscape designer and their workers. As they are designing the layout of plantings, and if you live in winter climes, this is the time to address any snow-drifting problems. Often these can be handled with small berms, scrubs, evergreens, and the like. It can make snow removal much easier.

Whatever way you choose to go, either with the general contractor alone or separately with a landscaper, there are a number of outdoor elements that you should address with your architect as early on in the planning process as possible. This is the time to activate the landscaping subcommittee. Below are some typical exterior areas that you should now plan in detail. All of these generally fit under the broad heading of exterior environment or landscaping around a church.

The first landscaping areas to consider are any that will be visible through clear windows (and even doors) from the sanctuary and nave of the church. This might include any sanctuary areas visible behind the altar, to its immediate sides, or along the sides of the nave. These highly visible areas become de facto part of the interior decor of the church itself. Do what you have to do to make these areas ones of seasonal beauty. Nothing can spoil a sanctuary or nave backdrop like an electrical transformer or a bare parking lot (undoubtedly complete with a rusty 1988 Oldsmobile sedan). This is not the background you want for community prayer and worship.

After these vistas, the largest of these other exterior areas is probably the parking lot(s). Many municipalities require a certain amount of plantings, islands, trees, and such, but often you have the choice of species. As the area is large this should be the initiation point for your landscape plan of trees, bushes, scrubs, plantings, and flowers. Since this area is perhaps the more distant from the building, the question of watering should arise. Are you planning a sprinkler system? If not, are there proximate water outlets for hoses? You will be spending some serious money for these plantings. How are they to be maintained? Will you need electrical outlets there for trimming? Now is the time to add them to your lighting standards in the parking lot and elsewhere.

While we are on the subject of parking lots and lighting, has the subject of artificial light pollution been addressed? This can arise from the parking lot itself, and from the headlights of cars there for nighttime services. Are there any local code issues with these two light sources? Are there any proximate neighbors that will be affected by car traffic at night? Do they need light shielding? Berms and plantings can be an attractive alternative to fencing (we gave our neighbors the choice, and they selected the plantings over solid fencing; it was also a great PR gesture). Then, how will the light standards be controlled? Will there be a timer or sensor system? All these are legitimate exterior building issues to be taken up and resolved with your architect and the landscape subcommittee.

Another lighting issue to consider is decorative, or accent, lighting. This type of lighting is directed onto the building to highlight one or more of its external features. Most common would be the building front, a steeple or tower, a cross, the upper structure, a colonnade, and such. By asking what is/are your most prominent building feature(s), you should be able to determine the area(s) to illuminate if you so choose.

The front of the new church is another potentially large and important area for the attention of the committee. Is there to be a front lawn? Are there to be plantings across the facade of the church? Is there a driveway or drop-off lane? How will this be decorated in the landscape plan?

We chose to not create a front driveway or drop-off as we wanted an unobstructed view of the church front from the street. As our church was very close to the street (a four-lane major city artery) and would be somewhat noisy, we decided to augment the front ceremonial doors (three sets of large oak doors set in an apsidal entryway) with a broad sidewalk. This was lined on the sides with flowers. In short order it became a new wedding custom for the fathers to present the bride and groom to the waiting guests flanking the broad sidewalk through these center doors. It is amazing how people, when well formed in the use and functions of a building, can create new traditions.

Since the front of the church was not to be the ordinary entry for the parishioners at weekend Masses (the street did not allow parking or standing), and since our parking facilities were on both sides of the building complex, it was important to give special attention in the landscaping and exterior environment to what would be the most common approaches to the new building. The transition to worship begins in the parking lot and is carried into the narthex or vestibule. So on the side of the new church with the larger parking lot we wanted an approach that would begin to put people into a mind-set for worship. This was an important discussion in the subcommittee. In fact it led to the creation of a devotional niche in the side wall and the placement of the patronal statue there. That and some strategic plantings softened the transition from work-a-day preoccupations into a spirit of communal prayer. I think it is important to consider these views and the psychology that goes with them. They are all significant in creating the worship experience.

Turning from the parking lots, driveways, and approaches, there are some smaller spaces that are a bit more exciting for your consideration and creativity. With the building of a new church, do you need a new church sign? Depending on the distance from the old to the new church, a relocation of signage might be necessary. The color of plantings and flower beds around it can draw the eye as long as they don't obstruct the sign itself. Generally, outdoor church signs should match the style and finish of the exterior of the building. I personally believe two-sided signs perpendicular or at an acute angle to the street for dual directional traffic provide the better visibility than a sign parallel to the street. You might ask your architect or landscape designer to draft something. Don't forget electricity for illumination (and an outlet here can be handy for trimming plants in this area, for Christmas lights, etc.). Tasteful trash receptacles by entrances and throughout the grounds are essential to litter management.

Are you blessed with bells? If they are real bells, will they need to be relocated to the new church building? Have the architects designed a location for them with the reinforcement needed to handle their weight? If they are electronic bells, where will the speakers be located for the new church? Be sure the architects design something to conceal the speakers yet allow them to be clearly heard in the directions you designate. If you are interested in new bells, the real kind, be prepared for a financial shock. The casting of new bells is very expensive. Another route is to attempt to find existing bells in structures that are no longer used or are scheduled for demolition. Your architect may be able to direct you in this search, or you can also check on the internet. If you are interested in new electronic bells, there are some superb CD systems available for a fraction of the cost of the real thing. Your acoustical engineer/consultant should be able to provide guidance in this regard.

Do you now have (perhaps attached to your school) or are you planning a flag display area? If this is to be a new area, you will need flags, flagpoles, and lighting if nighttime or around-the-clock displays are planned. We had had no exterior flag display but found that the parish scout troop (for the American flag) and the Knights of Columbus (for the papal church flag) were most interested in donating to this special project. Flag size and flagpole height should be determined by the adjacent proportions of the building. Our area was next to the church and adjoining one of our two parking lots, so we chose to add a bench to the display for passenger pickup. It made an attractive setting. Of course flag displays can be a single standard, a dual standard, as we did, or even a triple standard by the addition of a parish logo, patronal flag, or banner. Seek the guidance of your landscape design artist to ensure a tasteful and appropriate display.

Have you thought about a formal cornerstone? Inscribed with the name of the church and the date of construction, cornerstones (or monument stones) today can be mounted just about anywhere on the building. They no longer have to be actual corner supports. This is another outside element with which you can be creative. Do you want some emblem on the stone besides the name and date? Should it be mounted by the front doors, by a main entry if that is different from the front doors, knee level or eye level, similar to the exterior finish or a contrasting material? Should it contain a time capsule? Prepared by the school or the whole parish? Time capsules have a way of creating excitement and the potential of involving a number of people.

Depending on the location and timing of placement, a cornerstone-laying ceremony is an opportunity to bring people together at the building site for a time of prayer and celebration. Structure the prayer service, if it is done apart from the church dedication, to be one of gratitude for what has been accomplished so far, for the recognition that Jesus Christ is the true cornerstone of this structure, and for the blessings from God's hand for the work that remains that will stretch into times and ages for generations to come.

You are familiar with statuary from the previous chapter on artwork. Is there to be any outdoor statuary for your new church? Where will it be located? Will it require any alteration of the exterior of the building to accommodate it (our patronal statue was placed in a large niche in one of the outside apsidal walls)? What about lighting for night display? Other locations for outdoor statuary might include the sign area, the front entrance, a parking lot island, a pedestrian island of a sidewalk connecting other buildings to the church. Are there to be any water features (falls, fountain, reflecting pool)? Inground or aboveground? Surrounded by flower beds? Can this be combined with the statuary or near it?

One idea that arose for us was the idea of a contemplative prayer garden. This sprung from a number of sources: We had a triangle of land (approximately 2,500 square feet) behind the new church with adjacent trees and proximate to the parish offices. A couple of parishioners on the landscape subcommittee also raised the issue as a desire. And finally, I had noticed on trips to western Europe that many ordinary parishes had side gardens. Thus began a wonderful, creative project.

Working with our landscape designer we explored a number of concepts first. It was obvious from the start that the space was limited. This eliminated a long prayer path such as an outdoor Stations of the Cross or some other devotional walk. There was not enough room.

Also eliminated was the idea of a prayer labyrinth. Again, not enough space, although labyrinths can be inlaid in even a small courtyard. If you have the space available, give these popular outdoor prayer devotions some serious thought and discussion.

What emerged for us was a prayer garden. Shade is important and we were fortunate in that the building itself provided shade in the morning hours (the garden was on the west side) and afternoon shade was provided by a couple of older maple trees. Without trees you may want to look into a combination of arbors and trellises. Shade is essential if you want this to be a meditation area. Perhaps even a gazebo if the space will support it.

We provided three entrances to the prayer garden, marked by dual brick columns about four feet high. A plaque on each quoted Psalm 46:11, "Be still and know that I am God" (RSV), inviting people to enter, to quiet themselves, and to pray. Two pathways in paver bricks gently curved between the entryways and intersected each other. Along the paths were four brick columns about two feet square that narrowed as they rose to about five feet in height. On each column was a bas-relief plaque in bronze portraying a scene from Mark's gospel with a quote from the depicted passage below it. Across from each column was placed a two-person park bench for contemplation of the image and the quote. To one side were a small picnic-style table and benches for those who might want a table for journaling or reading.

The artist and subcommittee worked in conjunction with each other and chose these themes: healing, courage, faith, and God's will. They communicated back and forth with sketches, and the images and quotes that surfaced were of a gentle Jesus curing the paralytic man on his mat ("Child, your sins are forgiven," Mark 2:5); of a powerful Jesus walking on a storm-tossed bank of waves ("Take courage, it is I, do not be afraid," Mark 6:50); of a smiling Jesus standing behind a young girl, holding her hands up as she smiles with delight ("Everything is possible to one who has faith," Mark 9:23); of a kneeling and troubled Jesus leaning on a rock in the Garden of Gethsemane in prayer ("Abba, Father, all things are possible to you. Take this cup away from me, but not what I will but what you will," Mark 14:36). All of these were powerful and thought-provoking sculptures and Scripture quotes that enabled prayerful reflection. In the process, ownership became so strong among many members of the landscape committee that a permanent garden and flowers group arose to maintain and care for these outdoor features of the new church.

The exterior of a building and its environs are the public face of the structure. It is the first, and often the lasting, image of this church to the surrounding community. Focus and attention in these areas speak to the broader community of your understanding of the beauty of creation, while they also annunciate to your own faith community the prayerful dignity and nobility surrounding the house of the Lord.

## Chapter 18

# Construction Wrap-Up and Loans

While construction moves forward, there are a number of opportunities for celebration. Previously we have touched on the groundbreaking (chap. 14) and the laying of the cornerstone (chap. 17) as occasions for celebration. These events provide the faith community an opportunity to pray for the church, support the enthusiasm necessary for an ongoing building campaign, and celebrate significant building milestones along the way to completion. These are easily planned by the pastor and the steering committee along with the parish liturgy director. They are important connectors for the parishioners to the building as it materializes.

There are a couple of other possible celebrations that may not be as well known as the traditional groundbreaking and cornerstone ceremonies. Depending on timing factors—you do not want these events running too close together as that will dilute their impact—here are some other celebrations during the construction phase that you may want to consider using. Remember that a one- to two-year building project is a long time for most people who may be familiar only with the six- to eight-month construction time for a house.

In the construction trade, especially among ironworkers who erect the skeletal support structure, topping out is considered a significant event. This is the placement of the highest structural element of the building. In fact the ironworkers usually mark this event with their own ceremony (a U.S. flag, an evergreen sprig, and a small spool of wire attached to the last piece put in place). I think you can tie into this tradition for a celebration and ceremony of your own. Here's an example of what we did with it.

Our church was to have a large (55-foot) lantern steeple atop the intersection of the nave and the transepts. For safety's sake this steeple was constructed on the ground. When completed this 22-ton assembly was to be lifted by crane and put in place, topped off by a large gold-painted cross. All of this gave us the idea for a steeple-raising party.

This steeple-raising party was midweek, and we served champagne and hot dogs (because we are classy but with the common touch). Some volunteers grilled the hot dogs, and the champagne was supplemented with lots of sodas. We contacted the city to alert them to potential traffic hazards, and police officers were provided. First, the steeple was hoisted by a 160-ton crane. When that was in place, the base of the cross was signed by the workers, steering committee members present, staff, architects, and contractor representatives. The cross was lifted off the ground and blessed by me while I was standing on a telescopic boom platform complete with bullhorn and holy water. After the blessing the hoist was completed and the cross was placed atop the steeple. Then the champagne brunch was served to about two hundred onlookers who enjoyed all the events from blankets or lawn chairs that they had brought with them, as instructed. Although the celebration was done tongue-in-cheek, the prayer and blessing were most serious, focusing on the symbolic significance of this building with its steeple pointing to the heavens and its cross proclaiming the Christian message to all. Lots of pictures captured and communicated the event to the rest of the parish (and civic community) unable to be present. Although we did it as a steeple raising, a similar celebration could be held around the placement of a cross with no steeple, or with the mounting of a bell or bells, or for the final peak element.

Another occasion for celebration and parishioner involvement at the site is what I called the closing of the walls. The exterior walls and the shell of the church were virtually complete but many of the interior walls were yet to be put into place. I suspect they were left open for an inspection of some sort. Many of the structural steel beams, piers, and columns were still exposed. We took advantage of this one weekend after each of the Masses to invite the people to the building site to write their family names (and a prayer for the new church if they wished) on one of the beams before they were enclosed by the walls. This was enthusiastically received. We gave the general contractor plenty of notice after working out a time with him. The site was swept up as they left on a Friday to reduce the risk of tripping. Yellow caution tape was used to rope off hazardous areas and to create a circulation path. A number of black markers were hung by strings from various columns and posts for signing. The steering committee members were present to act as guides and to field any questions. Large numbers participated after each Mass. Excitement was high as this was their first look at the building from the inside. We designated approximate areas where the altar, tabernacle, baptistry, and the like would be located.

Again, this event kept up parishioner interest and connectedness to the project during the long building process. Besides signing beams and columns I have heard of parishes doing similar events by having the people sign the walls of a baptistry before it is tiled, or signing the subfloor around the altar (the predella) before it is finished with wood, tile, or carpet. This event, though not necessarily marked by direct prayer, begins the process of parishioner attachment to a new interior space for worship. Many of the prayers written on our beams along with the names were quite touching. One particular prayer printed by a nine-year-old child on one of the heavy steel I-beams was most poignant: "Dear God, please hold this up!"

As the construction phase begins to wind down there will be a number of inspections by architects, city building code officers, fire marshals, and the like. Actually, there have been inspections by various officials all along the way as the building developed (e.g., plumbing, electrical, fire suppression, etc.). These inspections, which relate to many safety issues, lead to a certificate of occupancy indicating that the public can officially take up the use of the building. This means that the structure is substantially complete.

Frequently there is still some work that continues after occupancy (even more if the occupancy permit is only temporary). The task that follows is known in the building trades as the punch list. This is a list of items that remain to be completed, are not right according to the specification, that may have been damaged during construction, or do not work properly. The punch list might include items as minor as some paint touch-ups, or as major as a malfunctioning heating or cooling system.

The formal punch list is usually composed by the architect (with the owner) and the general contractor during a walk-through of the building to test everything. Be sure to note painting and finish issues, floor coverings (loose or ill-fitting carpet, wood, tiles), electrical outlets and switches (test all; also test the breakers, and make sure they are labeled in a way you can understand), plumbing and fixtures, heating, cooling, and venting systems along with any timers and controls, and so on throughout the building. Things can be added to the punch list at the AOC meetings. Begin a list of your own and mark off items as they are addressed satisfactorily. Rather than relying on a single walk-through myself, I began to carry a pocket digital recorder and noted anything I saw or had questions about whenever I was in the building during the last weeks. A lengthy punch list does not necessarily reflect negatively on your contractor, as a building of this size and complexity is made up of many components that are installed by many different subcontractors and crews. The quality of your contractor (and his subcontractors) is reflected more in the manner and timeliness with which the punch list is addressed. Remember though, these take time and there are other jobs being addressed by all involved. Be patient and reasonable. The general contractor's motivation in this area is that the last 10 percent (5 percent if the punch list is small or mostly completed) of the contract money is usually withheld until these items have been completed.

Before making that final payment another thing you want to secure is the as-built drawings. This is a set of the plans that have been amended and annotated by the architect and the contractor, indicating anything that may have deviated from the original construction documents, either as bid or as altered in the value engineering process. This will be important for any follow-up work in future years. These should be filed in the parish archives (and most dioceses want a set for their construction and building archives as well).

With the final payment to the contractor you should receive all manuals for equipment in the church. I suggest you note the date of final completion (or installation/operation) as most warranties run from this time. Sort, file, bind, or do whatever is necessary to keep the manuals available for reference. Most contractors will schedule a time to go through the basic operation of systems in the new building with the owner, maintenance personnel, business manager, and whoever else you designate. Take notes and add them to the manuals.

Guarantees and warranties on most equipment have their own specific warranty time. Again, date and file all of these in case there should be a problem. The contractor's general warranty on the building usually runs for one year. When in doubt, refer to your architect and/or your diocesan construction and property person.

Let me turn now to the subject of finances and loans. There are two types of loans that will be needed for the financing of the new church building. The first is what I call the construction loan. This is the money necessary to pay for the total project cost (TPC; see expense listing in chap. 14) while pledges continue to come in. It is essentially a cash-flow loan. From the TPC you can deduct whatever savings you have on deposit with the diocese. Also you can deduct the pledge contributions that were paid up front during the capital fund drive and the ones that are coming in during the course of actual construction.

Let's take example 1, and say that your TPC for the new church is $6,500,000. Further, let's assume that you were able to accumulate $1,600,000 in savings from ordinary parish contributions over the years in anticipation of a building effort and before the capital campaign began. In this hypothetical example, let's say you raised $5,500,000 in pledges for a five-year capital fund drive. With a building amounting to $6,500,000 it looks like you have $600,000 extra to spend, right ($1,600,000 + $5,500,000 = $7,100,000)? Not so fast. Remember that your pledges are coming in over a span of five years while the building project will only take, say, eighteen months, at which time all costs are due to be paid. This is where the construction loan and its interest come in.

For the sake of this example let's say the capital fund drive received $1,000,000 in up-front contributions, and the rest ($4,500,000) spread out over the five years of the pledges, which is $900,000 per year or $75,000 per month. With construction costs of $6,500,000 being paid out over eighteen months (let's say evenly for the sake of the example—though it is almost never this neat—at $361,111 per month), then the $1,600,000 in savings plus the $1,000,000 up-front contributions plus the pledges paid in at $75,000 per month will run out at roughly nine months into construction ($75,000 × 9 = $675,000 + $1,600,000 + $1,000,000 = $3,275,000) ($361,111 × 9 = $3,250,000). This is when the construction loan would kick in.

The $3,225,000 construction loan is being paid by the $75,000 per month in pledges coming in. At 6 percent interest that loan would be paid out in forty-nine months of the fifty-one months (sixty months minus the first nine months of construction) remaining in the five-year pledges. This $415,190 in interest payments is where most of the leftover $600,000 is going. New pledges from families moving into the parish during the life of the five-year pledges hopefully will offset those pledges lost due to hardship, moving, or death.

*Example 1a:*

$6,500,000 – Total project cost (TPC)
- 1,600,000 – Savings accumulated before capital campaign
- 1,000,000 – Pledge contributions up front
- <u>   675,000</u> – Pledges paid during nine months of construction
($75,000 × 9)
$ 3,225,000 – Total construction loan
<u>+ 415,190</u> – Construction loan interest at 6 percent for
forty-nine months
$ 3,640,190 – Total paid, principle, and interest, for the
construction loan

There are loan payment calculators on the internet. Plug in your loan amount, the interest rate, and length (term) of loan. It should calculate for you the monthly payment, the total interest paid, and the cumulative total payments (principle and interest). You may be able to use this with the parishioners to encourage early pledge payments when possible. I have also included the formulae for your own spreadsheet calculator in appendix 18 (http://www.litpress.org/PDFs/new_church/appendix18.xls) where the monthly loan payment is known.

You can see that the construction loan interest has consumed most of the leftover $600,000. And you are still not finished. There is the *cathedradicum*. Some dioceses include capital funds (all or a percentage thereof) in the income of a parish that is figured for this diocesan assessment. If your diocese does not include this, count yourself most blessed. If the capital funds are included in the assessment, then take the amount of the capital pledges (received up front and yet to be paid), and multiply it by the assessment percentage. Remember that this is not due in a singular amount, but as the monies come in as revenue. So in this example the half million dollars is spread out over the five years of the pledge revenues, or about $100,000 per year apart from the up-front contributions given at the start of the campaign.

*Example 1b:*

$5,500,000 – Capital campaign pledges raised
<u>   × 9.25%</u> – Diocesan rate of assessment
$ 508,750 – *Cathedradicum*

The above example is predicated on a project whose cost, including the construction loan, virtually matches the capital raised (up front and pledged) in the fund drive along with savings already accumulated. Not all churches are this fortunate. Some new church building projects will have to assume what I call a mortgage loan in addition to the construction loan. What would this look like?

Example 2 is an illustration of such a situation. In this case we have a TPC of $8,000,000. For whatever reason (new parish, very rapid growth, little lead time) there is no advance savings on deposit. Enthusiasm is high in this growing parish, and the capital-fund campaign manages to raise $4,000,000 in pledges over three years. Of this $4,000,000 a fantastic $1,000,000 (25 percent) is contributed up front, many in lump sum payments. This means that the remaining $3,000,000 would come in over the three-year term of these pledges at roughly $1,000,000 per year ($83,333 per month). Let's say that the construction time is again eighteen months.

With construction costs of $8,000,000 ($444,444 per month for eighteen months), the $1,000,000 in up-front contributions and the incoming pledges of $83,333 per month would be exhausted in just three months ($83,333 × 3 = 250,000 + 1,000,000 = 1,250,000) ($444,444 × 3 = $1,333,332). This is when the construction and mortgage loan would begin at approximately $6,750,000. This loan would run for thirty-three more months, receiving $83,333 per month from pledge contributions. At the end of this total thirty-six-month period, the remaining principle would be approximately $4,975,830.

### Example 2a:

| | | |
|---|---|---|
| $8,000,000 | – | Total project cost (TPC) |
| -        0 | – | Savings accumulated before capital campaign |
| - 1,000,000 | – | Pledge contributions up front |
| -   250,000 | – | Pledges paid during construction period (three months) |
| $6,750,000 | – | Total construction loan |
| - 1,774,170 | – | Principle payments (+ $975,830 interest = $2,750,000) over thirty-three months |
| $4,975,830 | – | Mortgage loan balance at end of the three-year capital campaign. |

If you are obligated to a diocesan assessment for capital-campaign funds, you will need to figure $370,000 into this example, paid out over the three years of the pledge drive apart from the up-front gifts. I did not add this figure to the example since the assumption here was that this was a rapidly growing parish, and hence new families moving in would be able to make up this amount in added new pledges.

### Example 2b:

$4,000,000 – Capital campaign pledges raised
× 9.25% – Diocesan rate of assessment
$ 370,000 – *Cathedradicum*

So our example 2 parish still has a church building debt of just under $5,000,000. Now what? As the first capital-campaign drive was to build the new church, a second capital campaign is in order to pay off the existing church debt. In fact, most parishes have to run two or three capital campaigns to eliminate the cost of building a new church at today's prices. As this is a growing parish in example 2 that raised $4,000,000 in its first capital campaign, a second three-year campaign with a goal of $5,500,000 is not unrealistic. (Let's say $5,500,000 is raised; $1,250,000 is given up front; the remaining $4,250,000 is coming in over the three years of the second campaign at $118,056 per month; the loan would be paid out in thirty-five months.) And don't forget the *cathedradicum* on this second loan.

### Example 2c:

$4,975,830 – Mortgage balance going into second capital campaign
- 1,250,000 – Pledge contributions up front
$3,725,830 – Loan amount to be paid off at 6 percent interest over thirty-five months.

The two examples were given to show some of the more common parish situations: a parish with considerable savings versus one with no savings, a single five-year campaign versus two three-year campaigns back-to-back, and the importance of encouraging as many up-front contributions as possible to reduce borrowing costs. Whatever your parish situation, the essential message here is the importance of the calculation process and the inclusion of hidden costs like construction (or cash-flow) loans, mortgage loans, and any assessment (*cathedradicum*) costs. Be sure you, your office manager, or your finance person run these calculations early and often as numbers solidify. It can eliminate some nasty surprises later.

A parting word on finance and budgets. When preparing the first ordinary parish budget during which the new church will be occupied, it is important that you anticipate additional expenses in the areas of utilities, custodial services, grounds maintenance, supplies, and so forth, along with the interest, principle, and assessment payments. The last thing you want is to have to sacrifice ministries, programs, and services to make payments on a debt. Beginning early to figure and to anticipate these added costs can prevent such a potential difficulty.

*Chapter 19*

# The Dedication Ceremony

The Catholic liturgy for the dedication of a new church is an extraordinary ritual. (If you are of another denomination, please see your own ceremony here.) It stands out in that the primary focus is on a thing (a building and an altar) rather than on a person as in the sacraments. And yet it borrows heavily from the sacraments for its meaning and symbolism. The walls and the altar are sprinkled with holy water, a reminder of baptism and a sign of purification. Like the persons in baptism, confirmation, and holy orders, the walls and the altar are anointed with chrism, marking them as special and set aside for worship. This altar and these walls are enveloped in incense, a sweet cloud of prayer being offered up to God. Echoing baptism and ordination, the altar is wrapped in new clothing, festive garments fit for the sacrificial banquet table of the Lord. Once more recalling baptism, the altar is lit with candles, the light of Christ shining forth to all in this place.

This power-packed liturgy is the service by which this building is dedicated "solely and permanently," as the rite says, for the exclusive use of the faith community in its offering worship to God. This liturgy is led by the bishop and concelebrated by the pastor and other priests, deacons, and ministers. Generally it should be celebrated on a Sunday as the rite calls for a day when the most people can attend (a few days are excluded: Christmas, Epiphany, Ash Wednesday, Holy Week, the Triduum, Ascension, Pentecost, All Souls). The dedication is always celebrated with a Mass. The Scripture readings of the day are omitted

127

in favor of the texts that go with the rite (The Lectionary, nos. 701–6, with the first reading always being Nehemiah 8:1-4a, 5-6, 8-10).

Let me walk you and the steering committee through the rite of dedication (be sure to check with your diocesan office of worship or the bishop's master of ceremonies for dedication specifics). Then I will address some details and some suggestions. As we go through the rite and its various components be thinking about who should be invited to do these ministries. The temptation might be to fill the ministries at the dedication liturgy with steering committee or subcommittee members as they have worked the longest and hardest on this building. And that certainly is true. It is my opinion that at least half of those taking part in the dedication ritual should be chosen from the community at large. This is the entire building project's coming-out party. Spread the roles around, especially these most visible ones at the liturgy. You have worked hard through all these processes and consultations to make this a church built by the parish and not by a select few. Don't let it slip here at the last minute with a committee-dominated dedication ceremony. Involve as many people and segments of the parish as possible. Broad representation in the liturgy is not only good politics; it is good theology because it makes visible the variety of the people of God. There is a basic listing of the roles for a dedication liturgy in appendix 19 (http://www.litpress.org/PDFs/new_church/appendix19.pdf).

The liturgy of dedication offers three possible entry rites: a solemn rite with a procession to the church to be dedicated; a solemn rite without a procession; and a simple rite of entrance. These seem to be dictated mostly by the physical circumstances of your parish. The processional rite begins in another building and processes to the entry of the new church. This form of the rite requires a building space that can accommodate a large number of people. This could be the old church or what may have been serving as a worship space (a gymnasium or multipurpose building). In the case of a new parish split off an older one, the distance between the two may not make a procession feasible. It might be appropriate to hold a prayer vigil the night before dedication in the mother church (maybe using Evening Prayer I from the Office of the Dedication of a Church?). For parishes being consolidated into a new church, perhaps there could be vigils in each one at staggered times.

The second possibility is the solemn rite without a procession. Here, the people gather at the entry to the new church. This form seems to imply that there is not another building present or a building of adequate capacity to hold the people. This might be the case where a new parish is being established and the church is the first structure. The vigil the night before at the mother church from which the new parish is derived might be appropriate.

The third rite is the simple one, gathering the people in the new church with the bishop entering in a simple procession from the sacristy to the sanctuary. This form seems to imply inadequate space around the entry, unfinished surroundings at the entry, and/or inclement weather. I find it the least desirable symbolically, and I would avoid it at all costs, even if I had to rent and erect a tent for the gathering and procession.

Whatever entry form is used, the ceremony begins with a greeting to the assembled people by the bishop. After the greeting and exhortation the solemn rite calls for the bishop to begin the procession, accompanied by hymns, to the door of the new church. Without the procession the bishop and ministers are already at the doors or in the building at the presider's chair. Next comes the handing over of the building to the bishop. A small group of representatives (architect, contractor, supervisor, steering committee member) address the bishop and the people about the completed building, its features (size, number accommodated, design, artwork, or the like). They present to the bishop the official documents of the building (a copy of the plans, specifications, a list of the workers and supervisors, occupancy permit, and the like), along with the keys to it. (At our dedication we did all of the above in the old church before the procession to the new church doors because we had the people seated, there was good visibility, and there was a PA system for all to hear the handing-over procedure.) The bishop passes the keys to the pastor who unlocks the doors and the bishop invites all to enter.

At the chair the bishop blesses the water to be used first to sprinkle the people, then the walls of the building, and finally the altar. The Gloria and opening prayer follow. The Liturgy of the Word is celebrated with special texts for the occasion. The bishop's homily and the Creed happen next. The Litany of the Saints is sung in place of the general intercessions or prayers of the faithful and is concluded with a prayer by the bishop.

If relics (of a martyr or a saint) are to be used at the new altar, they must be placed beneath the table of the altar and not placed on or set into it. Following the Litany of the Saints, the bishop places the relics in the prepared opening beneath the altar table, and it is sealed by a stonemason or another workman. See the rite itself for other directions about the procession and disposition of relics up to this time.

The prayer of dedication, which specifically asks for God's blessings on this special place, follows the placement of the relics. This is a wonderful prayer, rich in images of the church, that could be beneficially unpacked for your people at any time before the dedication (the church—a house of prayer, a temple of worship, a home for sacramental nourishment, the bride of Christ, a virgin and a mother, a vineyard with branches embracing the whole world, the dwelling of God, built of living stones, founded on the apostles with Jesus as the cornerstone, a city on a mountain, a beacon of light, an echoing of prayer, its altar the table of sacrifice and nourishment, its waters of baptism the death of sin and a new life of grace for God's children, the memorial of the Lamb, the body and blood of Christ, a banquet of Word and sacrament, a place for the poor and oppressed, a city of peace for all God's people).

This prayer introduces the heart of the dedication symbolism. After proclaiming the prayer the bishop proceeds to anoint the altar with chrism and may invite two to four concelebrating priests (the pastor and others) to anoint the walls of the church after he has finished the altar. These anointings in the form of a cross may be at four or twelve places so designated in the church. Marking them with a candle and a permanent cross is an option. At our dedication, as the priests anointed the walls the bishop went to anoint the altar in the chapel.

Symbolic of the pleasing sacrifice of Christ ascending before the Father, a brazier (we used four) is processed in and placed on the altar, with incense added by the bishop with a prayer. As the smoke of the incense fills the church, the sunlight from the windows may create shafts of light. Incense is put in a censer for the bishop to incense the altar. Then the people throughout the sanctuary, and the walls, are incensed by concelebrants or ministers.

The altar is then wiped down (we had four people do this, processing with large, white towels, as if gently drying an infant) in preparation for being clothed. The altar cloths are placed and the new table of the Lord is decorated. Flowers may be placed around the altar and in the sanctuary area. Candles are arranged by the altar as is appropriate for the celebration of Mass. When in place, the bishop hands a taper to the deacon or minister to light them. All the lights of the church should be turned on as a sign of great joy, Christ shining forth.

The Liturgy of the Eucharist continues in the usual way with the presentation and preparation of the gifts. The preface for the dedication of a church is used, and if Eucharistic Prayers I or III are prayed, they have their own special forms for a dedication (I: "with heart and hand have given and built this church as an offering to you" . . . recall the chapel statue in Rouen; III: "may all your children now scattered abroad be settled at last in your city of peace"). Again, the preface itself is a treasure trove of images, echoing many of the themes of the dedication prayer. The Eucharist continues in ordinary fashion through the communion rite.

After communion is completed the inauguration of the Blessed Sacrament chapel (if there is no chapel, then the tabernacle itself) takes place. The ciborium or pyx containing the sacred species is left on the altar until the prayer after communion is completed. Then the bishop incenses the Blessed Sacrament and, carrying it with humeral veil, processes (with cross, candles, incense, and ministers) through the nave of the church to the chapel (tabernacle) as hymns are sung. The Blessed Sacrament is then placed on the chapel altar (in the tabernacle), incensed again, and, after a time of silent prayer, enclosed in the tabernacle. One of the ministers lights the sanctuary lamp, and the procession returns to the sanctuary for the bishop's final blessing and the dismissal. A concluding hymn is sung. An outline form of the key elements of the liturgy of dedication is found in appendix 20 (http://www.litpress.org/PDFs/new_church/appendix20.pdf).

The instructions with the rite of dedication call for the drawing up of a dedication record. This document is to include the date of dedication, the name of the bishop, the church's official title, and the name of the saint's relic, if used. This is to be signed by the bishop, the pastor, and community representatives. Copies are to be placed in the diocesan and parish archives. Check with your office of worship or the diocesan archivist if your diocese has a particular form for this document.

Having looked briefly at the rite of dedication, you can tell there are many details and arrangements to be attended to for such a special and important liturgy. Enlist the help of the diocesan office of worship, the bishop's master of ceremonies, your liturgy and music directors, and the steering committee to assist with these tasks. Let me suggest just a few reminders and ideas that may prove of assistance.

Obviously, the entire parish is invited to the dedication ceremony through the bulletin, newsletter, pulpit announcements, and on the parish web site. As the whole parish usually cannot fit into the new church at one service, it is suggested that the dedication liturgy be either the first or last Mass of the weekend (if last, use the old/former church for the earlier Masses). That way the parishioners can be provided for at the other services. In addition to the bishop, it is traditional to invite former pastors as well as deanery and area priests (as this is usually on a Sunday, they may need additional lead time in order to secure Mass coverage if they plan to attend). If civic invitations are in order for your local area, the city mayor, the county executive, and the like should be included by mail. It is wise to inform those invited, especially the parishioners, to expect a liturgy of at least two hours.

When it came to the worship aid for the dedication we chose to go with a rather simple, in-house printed program that included the sequence of the ceremony with very brief explanations of meaning (not all guests would have had the benefit of the preceremonial parish catechesis), the music, and prayer responses needed by the congregation. With the money saved we decided to put out a glossy, four-color dedication booklet with many pictures that outlined the journey of the parish to this new church. Included were a pictorial history of the early years of the parish and its first church; former pastors, associate pastors, and deacons; snapshots of parish life and events through the years; and details from the new church planning processes. Floor plans, elevation drawings, pictures of the committees at work fleshed out many of the tasks along the way. Then with artists' sketches and pictures, the story of the new building was told: the chapel, the tabernacle, the altar, and the many sanctuary furnishings, the symbolism of the four stained glass rose windows, the refurbished twelve apostles windows, the Stations of the Cross, the new statues, the prayer garden sculptures, the reliquary. The booklet closed with candid pictures of the elements of construction from the first bulldozer to the setting of the steeple's cross and everything in between (this is why you need to be so faithful to taking pictures whenever you visit the site). This keepsake booklet was printed by the company that did our church pictorial directory and was paid for by the pages of patron advertising in the back of the book. Hundreds were printed. Every family received one. Guests at the dedication and the open house were offered one. Others remain to this day (five years later, at the time of this writing) for those visiting the church who wish to know about the church's symbolism and its artwork. We felt that this twenty-eight-page booklet would be a more treasured and beneficial memento, and have a longer shelf life on family coffee tables, than a more elaborate and elegantly printed dedication worship aid.

Since space will be at a premium for the dedication, I suggest that you schedule an open house for the entire neighborhood, the civic community, area churches, and ministerial alliance members sometime shortly after the dedication itself. Invitations can be printed and mailed along with notices run in the local press and media. Something on the order of a Sunday afternoon, perhaps from 2:00 p.m. until 4:00 p.m., can be scheduled with tours and light refreshments. Steering committee and subcommittee members were enlisted to give the tours, grouping people as they arrived. They explained the various features, furnishings, and artwork of the building. Map out a route through the building and script some factual notes for the guides. The tour guests were invited afterward to the parish hall for cookies and coffee. I was surprised by the attendance and the interest. This turned out to be an excellent community outreach endeavor.

The rite of dedication itself, in its introductory notes (no. 20), calls for the pastoral preparation of the people "that [they] may take part fully in the rite." It suggests that they be prepared for the celebration by instruction regarding the spiritual, symbolic, and ecclesial meanings of the rite. With this in mind, I suggest at least one homily on the basics of the liturgy of dedication, around three weeks before the actual ceremony. For a sample homily outline see appendix 3.11 (http://www .litpress.org/PDFs/new_church/appendix3.pdf). The thrust here should be to help your people be focused for this symbol-filled liturgy.

The week before dedication, if you have not already done so, test all systems. You want no surprises on that day. Test the sound system and all microphones. Test the heating and air-conditioning systems, especially the air exchanger, as you will want to be able to clear the incense smoke efficiently. Note: turn off the smoke alarms that day, and alert the system monitors what you are doing and why. Nothing spoils the incensation of a new altar like an automatic sprinkler system! Test the bells (a nice touch to add to the Gloria or the lighting of the building). Tune the piano and other instruments. Check the organ. Be sure all toilets are in good working order. And finally know where all important switches are or have someone ready who does.

All music should have been chosen months ago and be familiar to the congregation by the time of dedication. You want hearty responses. This is not the time to introduce a new congregational piece. For the solemn procession to the new church, I suggest part of the choir remain in the old church (or other building) to sustain singing as the people exit, and part of the choir be in the lead with the people (arriving first) at the new church doors to sustain it as they gather. The same applies to the entry into the building, a part remains behind and a part enters first. A fading processional hymn at either place is a weak entry.

Let me close this chapter with one more practical suggestion for you and the parishioners. The move to a new worship space has the potential to create a fair amount of chaos and confusion. The people are being happily disrupted, but disrupted nonetheless. The patterns of years in the old church are now changing—where to park, where to sit, familiar pew-mates, etc. All of this has the potential to affect how the new church is initially perceived and accepted. So take the time to warn the parish. Better to anticipate than to presume. A homily a week or two before the actual move to the new building can work wonders in alerting people to the issues and psychology of the change, and asking for their patience with each other and themselves. Another homily three to four months after the dedication and move also might be in order to address any housekeeping details with the new church that you did not anticipate, now notice, or are hearing about. There are sample homily outlines in appendices 3.12 and 13 (http://www.litpress .org/PDFs/new_church/appendix3.pdf). We called these new church etiquette, and they were appreciated.

## Chapter 20

# Conclusion—Reflections

How to sum up the multiyear experience of building a new worship space for a faith community? Let me start on the lighter side. I recall an old, cantankerous priest a number of years ago who told the story of talking to the bishop at the time, saying that the seminary formation program was all wrong. Four years of theology was excessive, he thought. The bishop was intrigued as he himself was an educator and asked the veteran pastor what he thought the program for parish priest formation should be. "Well, your Excellency," he said, "they should fit all the Scripture, doctrine, and moral theology into the first year. The second year have the seminarians work for a buildings and property maintenance company so they learn how to fix plumbing, furnaces, and the like. The third year should be spent in a bank learning about finances." The old pastor paused, prompting the bishop to ask, "And the last year?" "Then the fourth year they should get a job as a ringmaster with Barnum and Bailey!"

After these years of assessment, planning, consultations, committee meetings, and actual construction you may justly feel you too have been in a three-ring circus. Even if you are a detail person you may have been overwhelmed with all the elements that go into a building and the decisions that have had to be made. You may have experienced the tension between processing it through the committees and the people or just deciding it yourself. The time and energy demands have been many. They may have taxed your limits. Undoubtedly there have been problems; there are always problems. With the structures and processes in place to handle them, they have been resolved, and without letting the problems themselves dictate the outcomes or behaviors along the way. You may have wanted to throw in the towel along the way, but you did not want to let down the Lord and his people.

So what have you learned? Again on the lighter side, I recall another pastor at the completion of his multiyear building project was quoted as saying, "Having learned everything there is about how to build a church, I have finally learned that I never want to do it again!" Perhaps a bit of exaggeration mixed with exhaustion for this pastor as most of us will only have to do this once in a lifetime. Another priest I asked said that he learned he was a better pastor than he was an architect. Hopefully you have learned what one priest termed "the appreciation of possibilities" that live within a faith community once they have been called to a vision, formed and informed, and activated. This is the ability of the people of God to rise to the occasion. It requires that you trust them, that you trust your staff, your committees, and the Spirit. And it requires that you be trustworthy—honest, patient, and thoughtful—if they are to entrust you with their community's future.

Along the way I hope you have learned the importance of your roles—convener, educator, and facilitator. The parish's ability to truly own this new church depended in large measure on these skills. The ability to articulate a vision, to call others together to test and flesh it out, to build consensus, and to facilitate the implementation into reality *is* the pastoral task, whether it is building a worship space or building a faith community. The church is best if it is theirs, not yours. That takes lots of involvement, prayer, communication, and celebration. Ownership is time-intensive up front, but pays huge dividends over the long haul.

The paradox I experienced was that I had set out to have the parish build their church, and in following all these processes, the new church built the parish. A community building for liturgy, prayer, and Eucharist built up the community's liturgy, prayer, and Eucharist. A community building built community. By empowering others, resolving conflicts, and honoring the processes, this building project became a very unifying event for the parish. If done well, building a new church can strengthen the communal bonds of a parish. If done poorly, it can be terribly divisive, and can be so for many years.

As a priest who grew up with the Second Vatican Council, I was imbued with the theology that the church was not its buildings, not bricks and mortar, that the church was the people. The process of building a church gave me a new appreciation for the role that a building does play in the life of a faith community. It is a source of pride and a crucial symbol of faith. Over and above any postconciliar iconoclasm, Catholics (and all Christians) are incarnational, and thus sacramental. The spiritual is incarnated in the material. A church of bricks and mortar embodies all the many and diverse elements of the community that occupies it. The church building as a symbol has a unique and privileged role to play. It is the tangible representation of the believers and their faith, of this community and its self-image. To use an Eastern theological term, the building is an icon.

Once you have built a church, a pastor once told me, you can never visit another church again in the same way. He said now when he is in another church he is attuned to the architectural features, the style and the themes, the details. And he asks himself what these things say about the community of faith. After building a church yourself you know firsthand what it takes of pastor and community to accomplish this task. You appreciate it all the more. When you look at the bricks and mortar, you see more. You see the people, the processes, and their efforts.

When you have been a pastor who has built a church you know how draining it can be emotionally, yet you should know how very satisfying it can be as well. I must say I enjoyed the vast majority of it all. It was fascinating to watch people's abilities blossom during the processes. It was intriguing to witness consensus emerge from discussions. And it was just plain fun to put on the hard hat and go out to see Bob the Builder.

Building a church is a privileged position for a priest and pastor. You have played a most significant role in the creation of this building. You are leaving a legacy from which generations will benefit. You have been part of molding and shaping a faith community in a once-in-a-lifetime way. You have facilitated their church for them. You have had an opportunity to articulate a theme of our Christian faith in a way that is unique to these people. You have risen to the challenge. You can now stand proudly among the church builders of the ages.

Along the way I hope you have enjoyed the process yourself, or at least most of it. Upon reflection—theological reflection—it should have told you some things about your parish, about your priesthood and pastorate, and about yourself. I encourage you to extend this same reflective experience to the members of your steering committee and the major subcommittees. A wrap party, as they say in the film industry, is in order. Invite the members to an evening of prayer and shared reflection. Help them to examine the spiritual meanings of which they have been a part. Encourage them to name the growth they have witnessed. Articulate the human and spiritual meanings of what you have shared together these many months.

Before the prayerful reflection adjourns and the celebration commences, here's an option for the future. Have someone videotape as many of the members as are comfortable sharing their insights. Invite them one-by-one to another room for their video interview. This is a wonderful way to preserve and archive these individuals and their thoughts for future generations. Imagine the impact of such a recording years from now at a parish anniversary celebration.

Let me close by saying that it is my sincere hope that you and your committee have found helpful ideas and practical suggestions within these pages. As one sayings goes, "Keep what you need; discard the rest." There are many successful church building projects. This is one approach among many. It was most rewarding for me and my parish. May you be so richly blessed in yours. I may be reached at jamesehealy@yahoo.com.

# List of Appendices

*Appendices are available online only and are downloadable free of charge at http://www.litpress.org/new_church.*

1. A Possible Steering Committee Structure

2. Demographic Formulae

3. Possible Homily Topics with Suggested Outlines

4. Architect Interview Form

5. Architect Interviews Compilation Form

6. Fund-raiser Interview Form

7. Fund-raiser Interviews Compilation Form

8. Strategic-Planning Survey

9. Acoustical Consultants Interview Form

10. A Sample Feasibility Study Questionnaire

11. Church Visits: Church Assessment Form with Design Guidelines

12. Church Visits: After-Mass Reflection Questions

13. Sanctuary Floor Plan: Some Geometry Reminders

14. Value Engineering Worksheet: Evaluations and Prioritizations

15. A General List of Church Furnishings

16. Artist Interview Form

17. Artist Interviews Compilation Form

18. Loan Calculation Spreadsheet in Format for Excel

19. A Basic Checklist of Ministries Needed for the Rite of Dedication

20. The Rite of Dedication from the Roman Pontifical